Christmas 2017
for
Kaitlyn
It's time to start
cooking! We can't
wait— to sample your treats!
Love,
Gram
C

Emma Lea's Family Cookbook

✎

Created by
Babette Donaldson
Author of *The Emma Lea Books*

Book design and production by
Patty Arnold, Menagerie Design and Publishing

Edited by
Bernice Wallace
Nani Nelson
Kathy Lio
✎

Enjoy your teas and Special treats.
Babette Donaldson

Published by BLUE GATE BOOKS

ISBN: 978-0-9792612-4-4

BLUE GATE BOOKS
P.O. Box 2137
Nevada City, CA 95959
530.478.0365

www.emmaleabooks.com   www.bluegatebooks

I dedicate this book to my mother.

In her kitchen I learned to the recipes handed down from my grandmothers
and great-grandmothers, an oral history of generations.
I still find comfort in preparing meals and joy in sharing them
with family and friends.

Contents

Teas

Making Tea With Children

by Babette Donaldson

It's usually the frills involved in tea that first attract young children; the teapot, cup and saucer, fun food. The tea itself — or whatever is served in the pot — is usually of less interest. But, as I visit schools and read the Emma Lea Books, I find people of all ages are interested in tea. They love the stories of countries where tea grows and the demonstrations of how loose-leaf teas return to their full leaf form as they brew the tea. Parents are especially interested when we discuss the healthy aspects of tea and become inspired to offer it as an alternative to canned sodas and sweetened juice drinks.

I like promoting tea I think it is wonderful to set aside a bit of time each day with family and friends to relax and share meaningful conversation. This is one of the common threads about sharing tea around the world. And I think it would be especially beneficial to children to have more tea times. I would like to see tea substituted for less healthful drinks. And I would like to help increase awareness of the way in which tea is grown around the world. Besides being healthy, tea is fun. Brewing and sharing it is easy.

So, just a few notes on preparing tea:

All kinds of tea, black, green & white come from the same kind of plant. Camellia sinensis. The flavors are different for many reasons. The plants are grown in different climates. The leaves are picked at different times of year. But mostly, the different flavors of tea are created by tea masters on each plantation who direct the picking and processing of the tea plants.

Herbal teas come from many different plants. Tea is one herb brewed as a beverage but there are many more. And they are combined by tea blenders to make thousands of flavors. When we say that a tea is an herbal tea, it means that leaves from the camellia sinensis plant has not been used. And the other herbs do not contain caffeine.

Black tea, plain and with added flavorings is brewed with very hot water. The water in the kettle should be boiling. And young children should not prepare or serve freshly brewed tea until it has had time too cool.

Green tea, plain and with added flavorings should always be brewed with hot water — but not boiling. You can remove the water from the heat just before it boils or add a bit of cold water to cool it. Green teas should not be left in the water to steep for long. Each tea has an optimum brewing time. You can experiment. But once your tea has reached your favorite strength, you should remove the bags or decant the tea from the teapot.

White tea, like green tea, should be brewed with hot water — not boiling. The same temperature of water can be used for white tea as for green tea. But it will not become as bitter if left to brew longer.

Most teas can be steeped at least two times. There is still a lot of flavor in the tea after the first infusion. Your own taste preferences will tell you how many times you can reuse your tea — and when to discard the leaves.

There are many different sweeteners and additives for tea. I recommend honey and agave nectar most frequently. Local honey has many added health benefits. And as organic sugars become more in demand, they are becoming more affordable.

Milk is very frequently added. Cream should not be used because the additional fat content coagulates and looks like skim on the top of the cup.

Lemon is also a popular flavoring for tea. But don't add both lemon and milk.

We've included several flavored tea recipes that children seem to enjoy. But I'm discovering great excitement when I take plain unflavored teas into school classrooms and allow them to taste premium teas from plantations around the world.

I'm often asked at what age children can begin drinking real tea because of the caffeine. And I always take a rather commonsense approach because each family's food preferences are so different. But any child already drinking caffeinated sodas will find tea to be much healthier — both because of the caffeine and the sugar content.

> The teapot is on, the cups are waiting,
> Favorite chairs anticipating,
> No matter what I have to do,
> My friend there's always time for you.
> An anonymous quote

Cambric Tea

There is an old custom of serving black tea with equal or greater amount of milk to young children at the family teatime. This is known as Cambric Tea, a light tea diluted with milk.

INGREDIENTS:

- Black tea, brewed light – OR – other favorite tea flavors
- Milk, heated
- Honey (optional)
- Cinnamon stick (optional)

DIRECTIONS:

Traditional Cambric Tea

Brew the tea and heat the milk. It is fun to serve a tea tray with pots of the tea and milk to be combined in the cup as it is served. In this way, the proportions can be individually adjusted. All amounts and proportions are to your personal taste.

Cambric Spiced Tea

Use a cinnamon spice tea or orange spice tea instead of plain black tea. Sweeten with a bit of honey and stir with a cinnamon stick. Allow the cinnamon stick to flavor the warm tea for 1–2 minutes as the tea cools.

Cambric Herbal Tea

Some herbal teas can be served Cambric-style. Rooibos and fruit flavors are some of the most popular herbals that blend with milk for a creamy taste.

Jelly Jar Tea

Makes 8 servings

I discovered this way of enjoying tea quite by accident. We were camping with limited supplies and unexpected guests. When the tea was brewed, there weren't enough cups to go around but a favorite jam jar was nearly empty. The solution seemed obvious. I later discovered that people had been sweetening their tea with jelly for many years.

INGREDIENTS:

- Your favorite tea
- Your favorite jelly

DIRECTIONS:

Brew your favorite tea. Add a spoonful of your favorite jam or jelly and stir. The jam or jelly sweetens the tea and adds the fruit flavoring. As you stir the tea in the jelly jar, you clean out the jar but you will probably want to serve it in either clean jars or in cute teacups.

ACTIVITY:

Collect different shapes of cute and unusual jelly jars. Allow each child to choose his/her own jar. Jars can be decorated with stickers and ribbons. Provide an assortment of jams and jellies for each guest to concoct their own special tea.

Iced Tea & Simple Syrup

If there is an U.S. Tea Tradition, it is brewed, iced tea. One popular story of the origin of iced tea is that a plantation owner, Richard Blechynden, was serving his tea on ice at the 1904 Worlds Fair in New York City on one very hot summer day. But food historians have also found mentions of iced tea predating this event.

- ❧ 6 teabags – or 6 teaspoons loose leaf tea
- ❧ 4 cups boiled water

Remove any strings and tags from the teabags. Place the tea in a heat-proof pitcher, preferably glass. Bring fresh, cold water to a brisk boil. Pour the water over the tea and allow tea to steep for 15 – 20 minutes. Decant the tea into another pitcher or storage container. Cover and refrigerate. Serve over ice. Optional, traditional garnishes are sliced lemons and mint.

Iced tea is delicious without sweeteners. But some favorites are honey, agave nectar, white and brown sugar or the simple syrup listed below.

Note: *Not every tea is as good iced as hot. Some teas turn cloudy when chilled, not affecting the flavor but much less appealing in the glass.*

Simple Syrup

- ❧ 2 cups sugar
- ❧ 2 cups cold water
- ❧ 1 tablespoon corn syrup

Boil 2 cups of sugar in 2 cups of cold water until the sugar crystals are completely dissolved. Remove from the heat and add corn syrup. Allow the syrup to cool at room temperature. When it is cooled completely, it can be poured into a clean glass jar with a tight-fitting lid and stored in the refrigerator.

Simple syrup is a wonderful way to sweeten iced tea and fresh lemonade. It can be served attractively in a small pitcher for your guests to sweeten their own beverages.

Southern Style Sweet Tea

Makes approximately 6 – 8 servings

Pre-sweetened iced tea is kept on hand every day and served throughout the day in a great many southern homes.

INGREDIENTS:

- 6 black tea bags
- 2 cups boiling water
- 1 cup sugar
- A pinch of baking soda
- 6 cups cold water

DIRECTIONS:

Place the teabags in a large glass carafe or mixing cup able to withstand heat. Pour the boiling water over the tea bags. Cover and steep for 10 minutes.

Remove the tea bags. Let them drip but do not squeeze them. Pour the tea mixture into a 2-quart pitcher; add the sugar. Stir to dissolve the sugar completely.

Add in the cold water. Let cool; chill in the refrigerator and serve over ice.

OPTIONS:

Add a sprig of fresh mint to the ice in the glass just before you pour the cold tea.

Garnish the rim of the glass with a lemon slice. Cut from the outside edge straight into the center — like a wagon wheel. Or, float the lemon slice on top of the tea.

Individual iced tea can be made by brewing a stronger cup of hot tea — use two teabags — then serving it over ice.

NOTE:

You can use almost any tea to make sweet iced tea. But, as noted on the previous iced tea recipe, some teas remain clear when you add the ice. Others become cloudy. This may not change the flavor but it does look less appealing. The addition of baking soda sometimes clarifies a cloudy tea.

Cranberry-Rooibos Tea

Makes 6 – 8 servings

INGREDIENTS:

- 2 cups brewed Rooibos tea
- 1 quart cranberry juice
- 2 cinnamon sticks
- 5 whole cloves
- Honey to taste

DIRECTIONS:

Brew the Rooibos tea. Combine all ingredients in a large saucepan. Simmer on low for 10 minutes.

Remove the spices and serve hot. If using unsweetened cranberry juice, you might want to add a bit of honey to sweeten the brew.

Your Notes

Orange Spice Tea

Makes 6 – 8 servings

INGREDIENTS:

- 6 tea bags, black tea
- 8 whole cloves
- 2 cinnamon sticks
- 1 cup apple cider
- 6 cups boiling water
- 1/2 cup sugar
- 1/2 cup orange juice
- Juice from 2 lemons

DIRECTIONS:

Boil the water and add tea, cloves and cinnamon. Remove from heat and cover. Let the tea steep for 5 minutes. Remove tea and the spices. Add the sugar and stir until completely dissolved. Add both juices and stir. The juice may cool the tea a bit too much. Reheat before serving, if necessary.

Your Notes

Matcha-Latte Tea

Makes 4 servings

INGREDIENTS:

- 4 rounded teaspoons matcha (Japanese-style, powdered green tea)
- 1/4 cup hot water
- 4 cups milk
- 4 tablespoons honey
- 2 drops almond extract

DIRECTIONS:

In a small bowl, add the hot water to the matcha and blend it well to moisten the tea and to break up any small lumps.

Heat the milk slowly, stirring constantly, being careful to keep it from burning.

Combine the hot milk and matcha in a blender container. You can use some of the warm milk to rinse the matcha from the mixing bowl. Add honey and almond extract. Blend it on a high speed to make it frothy. Serve immediately.

OPTION:

You can chill the mixture and blend it on high speed with 1 cup ice cubes for a frothy iced drink.

NOTE:

Matcha is a Japanese powdered green tea. It is made from tea leaves that have been grown under shade cloths to intensify the green color. Only the top leaves are chosen and are immediately dried and the whole leaf is ground into a fine powder. So, when we drink this tea, we are receiving the maximum health benefit from the tea plant. The antioxident value is one of the highest of any known food source.

Garden Mint Tea

Makes 4 servings

Mint is one of the easiest plants to grow. Actually, it is one of the most difficult to control once it takes root in a flowerbed.

INGREDIENTS:

- 4 cups water
- 4 sprigs of fresh mint
- Honey to taste

DIRECTIONS:

Wash the fresh mint thoroughly. Boil the water. Add the mint and boiled water to a heat-proof pitcher. Steep for 3 minutes. Remove the mint and stir in honey while it is still warm.

Mint is well known as a calming herb, perfect to enjoy before bedtime. It also helps settle a queasy tummy.

Other fruit and herbs blend well with mint. You can try adding other flavors to the water to steep with the mint leaves.

Delicious served both hot and cold.

Your Notes

Hibiscus Lemonade

When you combine freshly-squeezed lemonade with a tangy hibiscus tea, you have a lovely and unusual pink punch, perfect for a party.

INGREDIENTS:

Lemonade Ingredients:

- 2cups lemon juice *(approximately 10 – 12 large lemons)*
- 3 cups water

Simple Syrup Ingredients:

- 1 cup granulated sugar
- 1 cup water

Hibiscus Tea ingredients:

- 2 quarts water
- 1 cup dried hibiscus petals
- 1 cup sugar

DIRECTIONS:

Lemonade Directions:
Put the sugar in a small saucepan and cover with the water. Place over medium heat and stir until the sugar is completely dissolved. Boil for 5 minutes. Remove from heat and cool. Mix the lemon juice, water and simple syrup together in a large pitcher.

Hibiscus Tea Directions:
Bring the water to a full boil in a large saucepan. Add sugar and stir to dissolve. Remove from heat. Add the hibiscus. Cover the pot and let the tea steep for an hour. The color should be a deep red and the flavor will still be slightly tart. Strain the tea from the hibiscus petals into a large pitcher and refrigerate.

Serving:
The Hibiscus Tea and Fresh Lemondade can be mixed in advance or served separately for the guests to blend their own. Serve with ice. Garnish with think lemon slices floating on the top of the glass or cut from peel to center and slipped upright onto the edge of the glass.

Lemon, Ginger & Honey Tea

Makes 4 servings

INGREDIENTS:

- 1/4 cup peeled and sliced fresh ginger
- 1 fresh lemon
- Honey

DIRECTIONS:

Boil the fresh ginger slices in 3 cups of water. Reduce the heat to a low simmer for 10 minutes. Slice the lemon into quarters and squeeze the juice into each cup. For a little extra lemon flavor, drop the lemon into the cup. Pour 1/2 cup of the ginger water into each cup. Add a spoon of honey — to taste. Stir until the honey is dissolved. Add 1/4 cup of warm water. Remove the lemon before serving.

This is also very soothing for a sore throat.

From "Winnie The Pooh and the Honey Tree"

by A.A. Milne

"That buzzing noise means something. Now, the only reason for making a buzzing noise that I know of is because you are... a bee! And the only reason for being a bee is to make honey. And the only reason for making honey is so I can eat it." . .

. . says Winnie The Pooh

Homemade Chai

Makes 4 servings

A mortar and pestle can be fun kitchen gadgets and grinding is a good job for your young chef-in-training.

INGREDIENTS:

- 2 teaspoons crushed cardamom seeds
- 4 teaspoons crushed cinnamon stick
- 8 whole cloves, crushed
- 2 tablespoons grated fresh ginger
- 4 tea bags — black tea
- 2 cups water
- 2 cups milk
- Honey to taste

DIRECTIONS:

Remove the outer pods of the cardamom seeds and crush the remaining seed, the cinnamon stick and the whole cloves with a mortar and pestle.

Heat all ingredients together in a saucepan with low heat for 10 minutes. Strain and serve.

GREEN TEA CHAI:

Substitute your favorite green tea. Remember to brew green tea with slightly cooler water just before it boils. If you want it to be very strong, use more tea. Do not increase the water temperature or the length of time the tea steeps.

HERBAL TEA CHAI:

Substitute your choice of herbal tea; rooibos, mint, orange or other favorite herbs.

Red Velvet Cream Tea

Makes 4 servings

The creaminess of this tea comes from the gelatin. It makes a smooth, rich drink without the heaviness of real cream.

INGREDIENTS:

- 4 cups milk
- 4 Rooibos teabags
- 1 teaspoon unflavored gelatin
- 2 teaspoons cold water

DIRECTIONS:

Heat milk and teabags in a saucepan over very low heat for 10 minutes. While the milk is heating, dissolve the gelatin in cold water.

Add spoonfuls of warm milk to the dissolved gelatin gradually and whisk after each addition. Repeat this until the gelatin mixture is creamy. Then place the milk and gelatin into a blender and whip the mixture until frothy. Serve immediately.

For a party treat, you can decorate with a whipped cream topping and colored sugar sprinkles.

Rooibos-Red Bush

Rooibos, also known as Red Bush, is an herb grown in South Africa. The brewed tea is a beautiful red color and the aroma is floral. It is believed to have many health benefits and is served as a tea to babies who are suffering from colic and to the elderly to aid with digestion. But it is also used in beauty products and has many nutritional benefits. The flavor is naturally sweet and is becoming a popular herbal beverage. It contains no caffeine.

Tea Nog

Makes 8 servings

When the traditional holiday Eggnog recipe seems a bit too rich, try this variation. It's a favorite for winter parties.

INGREDIENTS:

- 8 black tea bags
- 1 cup boiling water
- 14 oz sweetened, condensed milk
- 4 cups whole milk
- 1/4 teaspoon ground nutmeg
- 2 eggs, well beaten
- 1 teaspoon vanilla extract
- Whipped cream
- Ground nutmeg

DIRECTIONS:

Steep all 8 tea bags in the cup of boiling water for 5 minutes to form a tea concentrate. Remove bags. Heat the condensed, whole milk and 1/4 teaspoon nutmeg to scalding.

Gradually add beaten eggs, tea, vanilla and salt. Keep on low heat for five minutes, whisking frequently Mix well and serve topped with whipped cream and a dusting of nutmeg.

OPTION:

A quick Tea-Nog can be made by steeping a favorite flavor tea in a commercially prepared eggnog. Adjust the amount of tea concentrate to your taste.

Herbal Tea Smoothie

Makes 4 – 6 servings

INGREDIENTS:

- 2 cups boiling water
- 6 teabags – your favorite fruit-flavored herbal tea
- 2 banannas
- 2 cups vanilla ice cream or flavored yogurt
- 2 tablespoons vanilla protein powder
- 8 – 10 ice cubes
- 2 cups fresh fruit (*such as strawberries, peaches, blueberries or nectarines*)

DIRECTIONS:

In a heatproof pitcher, pour the boiling water over the teabags and steep for five minutes. Remove teabags and refrigerate for at least 30 minutes or until well chilled. In a blender, combine the tea, banannas, ice cream or yogurt, protein powder and ice cubes. Blend on high speed until smooth – no large chunks of ice. Add fresh fruit and blend on a lower speed until it is ready to drink.

Cranberry-Chai Cooler

Makes 4 – 6 servings

INGREDIENTS:

- 2 cups boiling water
- 4 chai flavored teabags
- 2 tablespoons sugar
- ½ cup dried, sweetened cranberries
- Club Soda or other sparkling water, chilled

DIRECTIONS:

Steep tea for 5 minutes. Remove tea and add cranberries. Refrigerate for 15 minutes. Whirl the chilled mixture in a blender. Fill glasses with ice, and some of the tea mixture. Glass should be about half full. Top off with club soda and stir.

Wassail Tea

Makes 12 – 16 servings

INGREDIENTS:

- 2 cups of sugar
- 4 cups of water
- 6 tea bags, black tea
- 10 whole cloves
- 4 whole cinnamon sticks
- 1/4 cup sliced fresh ginger
- 3 allspice pods
- 2 cups orange juice
- 2 cups lemon juice
- 1/2 gallon apple cider

DIRECTIONS:

Simmer the sugar and water together for 15 minutes in a saucepan large enough to hole the remaining juices. Keep the heat at a level where the syrup bubbles gently but does not come to a rolling boil. Remove from the heat and add the tea and the whole spices. Cover and allow the tea to infuse in the syrup for 10 minutes. Remove the tea bags but leave the spices. Cover and let sit for 1 – 2 hours or overnight so the flavors infuse into the syrup.

Scoop the spices out with a slotted spoon. Reheat the syrup to a boil. Add the juices and heat it to a comfortable serving temperature. Serve immediately.

Here We Come A-Wassailing

Here we come a-wassailing
Among the leaves so green;
Here we come a-wand'ring
So fair to be seen.

Love and joy come to you,
And to you your wassail too;
And God bless you and send you
A Happy New Year
And God send you a Happy New Year.

God bless the master of this house
Likewise the mistress too!
And all the little children
that 'round the table go

Love and joy come to you,
And to you your wassail too;
And God bless you and send you
a Happy New Year
And God send you a Happy New Year

Apple Pie Tea
Makes 5 – 6 servings

TEA INGREDIENTS:

- 1 can apple pie filling (21 ounces)
- 1 cup milk
- 4 cups brewed Rooibos tea
- 1 cup apple cider

TOPPING INGREDIENTS:

The topping is optional but adds to the festivities.

- 1 teaspoon apple pie spice
- 1 cup whipping cream
- 2 teaspoons apple cider

TOPPING DIRECTIONS:

Prepare the topping by whipping the cream with electric mixer or hand whisk until it forms peaks. Mix in 2 teaspoons of the apple cider and the teaspoon of apple pie spice. Set it aside in the refrigerator until the hot drink is ready to serve.

Another decorating option is to cut a thin cross-section of the apple and let it float on the surface with a sprinkle of the spice mix or cinnamon. The apple softens a bit with the tea.

TEA DIRECTIONS:

Brew the cup of Rooibos tea (plain or flavored). Let it cool slightly. Blend the apple pie filling in a blender on a low speed until smooth and creamy. Gradually add the milk, tea and apple juice. Pour the mixture into a saucepan and heat over low heat until steamy but not boiling. Serve in teacups or mugs. Add the topping (if desired) and serve immediately. The whipped topping melts quickly in the tea.

A was an Apple pie;

B bit it;
C cut it;
D dealt it;
E eat it;
F fought for it;
G got it;
H had it;
J joined it;
K kept it;
L longed for it;
M mourned for it;
N nodded at it;
O opened it;
P peeped in it;
Q quartered it;
R ran for it;
S stole it;
T took it;
V viewed it;
W wanted it;
X, Y, Z, and all wished for a piece in hand.

An Old English Rhyme

Make it My Way Tea Party

The tea blending party can be a great rainy day activity or a tea party.

INGREDIENTS:

A trip to the health food store will offer you many herbal tea choices:

- Rose Hips
- Rose Petals
- Mint
- Rosemary
- Chamomile
- Lemon Balm
- Hibiscus
- Slivers of lemon and orange peel
- Dried blueberries and cranberries

EQUIPMENT:

- Fill-it-yourself teabags or individual teapots with infusers.
- Pencils and notepaper
- Measuring spoons

DIRECTIONS:

Have separate bowls of each ingredient. Encourage experimentation. Use small measuring spoons to create your own unique flavor combinations and make notes about your blend. Then, as you taste, make notes so that you remember your favorite recipes.

If you're having a party with several guests, you can share the different teas by pouring small amounts into each person's tasting cup.

There are many more flavors you might want to try to create your own teas. A trip to your local health food store is a good place to begin selecting herbals to make infusions. But growing herbs in your own garden is great fun. And you might experiment with unusual flavors. One company in France blends tea with vegetables like zucchini and sun-dried tomatoes. You'd be surprised by the flavor!

Your Special Tea Blend

Ingredients & How Much

What does it taste like:

Notes on your tea:

Cookies

Mending Hearts Cookie Game
Matcha Mint Cookies
Green Tea Leaf Cookies
Biscott-Tea Cookies
Rooibos Tea Cookies
Laura's Prize Winning Cookies
Oat-Tea Raisin Cookies & Raisin Glaze
Queen of Hearts' Tarts
Gingerbread People
Almost Too Much Ginger Cookies
Marmalade Cookies
Chocolate Cracker Cookies

Mending Hearts Cookies

Makes 24 – 36 hearts

This is an activity recipe. The recipe is a simple sugar cookie that is cut into heart shapes and then "halved" before baking. Each half-cookie is given to one of the participants. The object of the game is to find the matching half cookie.

INGREDIENTS:

Cookies:

- 3/4 cup butter, softened
- 1 cup sugar
- 2 eggs
- 1 teaspoon vanilla
- 2 1/2 cups all purpose flour
- 1/2 teaspoon salt
- 1 teaspoon baking powder
- Extra flour for rolling and cutting
- Parchment baking paper
- Heart-shaped cookie cutters
- Toothpicks

Frosting:

- 2 cups sifted confectioners sugar
- 1/2 cup butter
- 1 teaspoon vanilla extract
- 1–2 tablespoons milk
- Optional: Sprinkles, colored sugar crystals, food coloring

DIRECTIONS:

Cream the butter and add sugar, beating until the mixture is smooth. Add the eggs and vanilla and continue beating. Add the flour and salt and stir until the dough is smooth. It will be a thick dough so once you add the flour, you may want to finish with kneading it by hand. Wrap the dough in plastic. Refrigerate for about one hour. Line your baking sheet with parchment paper.

Lightly flour the board and rolling pin. Roll the chilled dough to your desired thickness – about 3/8". The thicker cookies are easier for children to use in the game. Cut the whole hearts and place on the lined baking sheets. Excess dough can be pressed into a new ball and re-rolled for another batch of cookies, but rolling too much excess flour into the dough can make them tough.

Tip: It is easier to cut the hearts if, after you roll the dough, you place it on the lined baking sheet and then chill the entire pan in the refrigerator for about 15 minutes. You can cut the cookies directly on the parchment and peel away the extra dough, leaving the cookies on the sheet, ready to pop into the oven.

Preheat oven to 350 ° F.

You and your child helper can use a toothpick to "draw" your cutting lines on each heart. Make each heart different. An adult can deepen the cutting lines with the pointed end of a sharp paring knife. But do not separate the halves. They will bake together but you can easily make the final cut when they come out of the oven. It helps to re-chill the raw cookies for 5 minutes prior to baking to help them keep their shape during baking.

Bake for 10 minutes until brown around the edges. Cool on the pan before separating the halves. Leave them un-frosted and make sure they're completely cooled if you are going to use them as a party game.

Frosting:

Cream the butter, sugar and vanilla together. Add small amounts of the milk and mix to the desired consistency. One drop of food coloring will add an optional bit of interest to the cookies and they can be topped with sprinkles of your choice.

If you're playing the game below, you may want to have the children locate their matching half and decorate them together.

THE ACTIVITY:

Choose enough cookie halves so that you have exactly enough for a half cookie per guest so that every cookie has a match. Mix them well on the platter. When your guests have all arrived, each one will choose one half heart. They will then try to find the match. When they find their other half, they must discover something about the other person they didn't know before. Then they can decorate their cookies as a team. Or, you may want to have fresh whole heart-shaped cookies to decorate and eat. Sometimes during the game, young children break the half-heart cookies.

Matcha Mint Cookies

Makes approximately 36 cookies

INGREDIENTS:

- 1 1/2 cups confectioners sugar
- 1 cup butter, softened
- 2 teaspoon dried, crushed mint
- 2 cups all-purpose flour
- 2 tablespoons Matcha (powdered green tea)
- 1 egg
- 1 teaspoon almond extract

DIRECTIONS:

Preheat the oven to 350 ° F. Line a baking pan with parchment paper.

Cream the butter in a large mixing bowl. Gradually add the powdered sugar to the creamed butter until well blended.

Add the egg and mix thoroughly. Add almond extract, matcha powder and mint. Mix well. Add flour gradually. The batter will be stiff. Chill in the refrigerator until firm.

Dough can be formed into small, walnut-sized balls and placed on parchment. They will flatten slightly as they bake.

Bake for 12–15 minutes, or until slightly golden around the edges.

Matcha Note:

Because Matcha has such high anti-oxident value, we've included seveal recipes with it as an ingredient. You can purchase Matcha from Asian grocery stores or specialty teashops. There are currently many online tea businesses that sell Matcha and other specialty teas.

Green Tea Leaf Cookies
Makes approximately 2 dozen cookies

INGREDIENTS:

- 1 cup all purpose flour
- 1/4 cup sugar
- 1/4 cup powdered sugar
- 1 tablespoon green tea (matcha) powder
- 1/4 teaspoon salt
- 1/2 cup butter, cubed
- 1/2 teaspoon vanilla
- 1 teaspoon water

DIRECTIONS:

Mix all the dry ingredients in a medium sized bowl. Cut in the butter until mixture is crumbly. Add vanilla and water. With your hands, knead it into a stiff dough.

Roll the dough into an oval log. Stretch it lengthwise on a sheet of waxed paper. Press one edge of your oval log down to a point so that the log creates the shape of a leaf. Wrap your "leaf shaped log" in waxed paper or plastic wrap and chill for at least 30 minutes if you're planning on baking immediately, or freeze the dough until you're ready to bake.

Preheat oven to 350 ° F.

When chilled, slice the log into 1/3 inch thick pieces. Score leaf designs in the top with a toothpick. Place on baking sheets and bake until the edges are just brown, about 12 minutes. Let cool on sheets for 5 minutes, then transfer to wire racks.

> "If man has no tea in him,
> he is incapable of understanding
> truth and beauty."
>
> Japanese Proverb

Biscott-Tea Cookies

Makes 36 cookies

Biscotti are cookies baked in a two-step baking process.

These are recommended for dunking in a cup of tea or a glass of milk.

They are a bit firm to eat without softening, but they do keep well and make

great "from the kitchen" homemade gifts.

INGREDIENTS:

- 1 cup raw almonds
- 1 teaspoon baking powder
- 1/8 teaspoon salt
- 2 cups all-purpose flour
- 4 teabags, Earl Grey or your favorite flavor
- 3/4 cup sugar
- 3 large eggs
- 1 teaspoon vanilla
- 1 teaspoon almond extract
- 1 cup boiling water
- Olive Oil

DIRECTIONS:

Preheat oven to 350 ° F.

Toast almonds for 8–10 minutes. Let cool and then chop coarsely. Set aside.

Moisten the teabags in the boiling water, about 1 minute. Remove from the water, open the teabags and remove the tea leaves so they can dry a bit.

Reduce oven temperature to 300 ° F and line a baking sheet with parchment paper. Waxed paper can also be substituted for baking parchment.

In a small bowl, lightly beat the eggs and extracts together. Set aside. Combine the flour, sugar, baking powder and salt in a mixing bowl. Whisk together until blended. Make a well in the center of the dry ingredients. Add the egg mixture and beat until it forms a stiff dough. Then add tea leaves and almonds by kneading them into the dough with floured hands. Divide dough in half.

On a lightly floured surface roll each half of dough into a log about 10 inches long and 2 inches wide. Position the logs on the prepared baking sheet, spacing the logs about 3 inches apart. Bake for 35–40 minutes, until firm to the touch. Remove from oven and let cool on a wire rack for about 10 minutes.

Transfer logs to a cutting board and, using a serrated knife, cut log into slices 1/2 inch thick on a diagonal to make each cookie a bit longer. Arrange evenly on the lined baking sheet. Brush both sides of the biscotti with olive oil. Bake 10 minutes, turn slices over, and bake another 10 minutes. Remove from oven and let cool. Store in an airtight container or freeze for up to two weeks.

ACTIVITY:

Make a batch of these cookies as a gift. Fill canister or jar and decorate with ribbon, fabric or paint. The cookies can be combined with some tea and a teacup. Be sure to include a note that they are real "tea" cookies.

I Saw Lu Yu off to Pick Tea at Tien Mu Mountain

Thousand mountains greeted my departing friend
When spring tea flourishing again
His profound knowledge about picking tea
Through morning mist or twilight clouds
That solitary journey has being my envy
Rendezvous in a temple of a remote mountain
We enjoyed picnic by a clear pebble fountain
In this silent night, Lit a candle light
Knocked a marble bell for chime
While deep in thought for old time.

by Huang Pu Zhen—Tang Dynasty poet,
friend of Tea Sage Lu Yu

Rooibos Tea Cookies

Makes approximately 18 cookies

INGREDIENTS:

- 1 teaspoon Rooibos herbal tea leaves
- 1/4 cup boiling water
- 1/2 cup buttermilk
- 1/2 cup butter, softened
- 3/4 cup brown sugar, packed
- 1 egg
- 2 teaspoons finely grated orange peel
- 2 cups all-purpose flour
- 1 teaspoon baking powder
- 1/4 teaspoon baking soda
- 1/4 cup powdered sugar (optional)

DIRECTIONS:

Infuse the Rooibos with the boiling water. Cover the cup and allow it to sit until completely cooled.

Preheat oven to 350 ° F.

In a large bowl, cream together the butter and sugar until light and fluffy. Beat in the egg, then stir in the Rooibos tea and buttermilk. Combine the flour, baking powder and baking soda and blend into the creamed mixture. Drop by rounded spoonfuls onto the un-greased cookie sheets.

Bake for 8 to 10 minutes in the preheated oven, until the edges are light brown. Allow cookies to cool on baking sheets for 5 minutes before transferring to a wire rack to cool completely.

Dusting with powdered sugar is decorative. It is optional.

Laura's Prize-Winning Cookies

Makes 18 – 20 cookies

INGREDIENTS:

- 1/2 cup butter
- 1/2 cup brown sugar
- 1/2 teaspoon vanilla
- 1 cup flour
- 1/4 teaspoon salt
- 1 cup finely chopped walnuts
- Jam or preserves, your favorite flavors

DIRECTIONS:

Preheat oven to 350 º F.

Mix all ingredients together except jam/preserves. Form into 1 inch balls and bake on a greased baking sheet at for 10–12 minutes. Remove from oven.

While still warm, lightly press a spoon into the cookie to make an indentation. Let cool completely.

Spoon jam/preserves into center of each cookie. You can use several different flavors of jam as filling for the cookies to serve at a party.

Recipe contributed by Amy Lawrence of An Afternoon To Remember, *Newcastle, CA*

Oat-Tea Raisin Cookies

Makes approximately 3 dozen small cookies

INGREDIENTS:

Cookie Dough:

- 1 cup raisins
- 4 spiced tea teabags (*black tea works well)*
- 1 1/2 cup water
- 1 cup of butter, softened
- 1 cup brown sugar
- 2 eggs
- 1 teaspoon vanilla extract
- 1/2 teaspoon salt
- 1 1/2 cups all-purpose flour
- 1 teaspoon baking soda
- 1 1/2 teaspoon cinnamon
- 1 cup chopped walnuts
- 3 cups quick oatmeal

Raisin Tea Glaze:

- Reserved tea from soaking the raisins
- 1 tablespoon butter
- 1 teaspoon ground cinnamon
- 1 cup powdered sugar

DIRECTIONS:

Cookie Dough:

Boil the water. Add teabags and raisins, cover and steep for 5 minutes. Remove teabags and save them. Keep the raisins soaking in the tea until cool. Then drain the raisins. ** Take the tea out of the teabags and discard the paper wrapper. The tea can dry on paper towel or in a colander.

Cream together the butter and sugar. Add eggs and vanilla. Mix well. Sift together the dry ingredients; flour, soda, cinnamon and salt. Fold in to the creamed mixture. Finally, add the oatmeal, walnuts, drained raisins and tea leaves.

Note: *Be careful to drain excess liquid from raisins and tea leaves. They should be moist but not "dripping". Chill dough for 2 hours or overnight.*

Baking:

Preheat oven to 350 ° F.

Scoop balls of cookie dough with a tablespoon onto an un-greased cookie sheet or baking parchment.

Bake for about 12 minutes — until edges and bottoms are golden but centers are still slightly soft. Remove from oven but let them sit on the cookie sheets for 5 minutes before moving.

** The decorative glaze makes these cookies more festive. The tea used to soak the raisins can be reserved and used to create a spicy glaze for the cookies.

Raisin Tea Glaze:

Simmer the liquid to reduce – about 5 minutes. This should leave about 1/4 cup. Add the butter and stir until melted. Add this to the powdered sugar and cinnamon. Stir until the sugar is dissolved.

"Tea tempers the spirit and harmonizes the mind, dispels lassitude and relieves fatigue; awakens thought and prevents drowsiness."

Lu Yu, 5th Century Chinese Poet

Queen of Hearts Tarts

Makes 6–8 small heart tarts or one large heart-shaped tart pan

This tart has a cookie crust which is a bit more fragile than a piecrust. If you have individual tart pans or baking molds, each child can press the dough into their pan. But this recipe can also be made as a single whole tart in a pie or cake pan.

INGREDIENTS:

Tart crust:

- 1/3 cup powdered sugar
- 3/4 cup cornstarch
- 1/8 teaspoon salt
- 1 cup all-purpose flour
- 1 cup butter (no substitutes)

FILLING:

- 1 basket fresh strawberries
- 1 cup strawberry jam
- 1/4 cup powdered sugar
- Individual sized heart-shaped baking pans or a larger heart pan. **

DIRECTIONS:

Sift together dry ingredients. Cut in the butter until crumbly. Gently work into a soft dough. Chill the dough for at least 2 hours.

FILLING:

Wash and remove the stems of the fresh strawberries. In a medium sized mixing bowl, crush the strawberries with a fork or pastry blender. Add the strawberry jam and stir well. Refrigerate until the crust is baked.

BAKING:

Preheat oven to 375 ° F.

You can bake these in special heart-shaped individual tart pans, muffin tins or a cake pan. Press the chilled dough into your choice of un-greased pan. Cover the bottom of the pan and let it come up slightly around the edges.

Bake for 7–10 minutes, until edges begin to brown. Spoon the strawberry filling into the crust immediately. Let them cool. You can dust with sifted powdered sugar before serving.

Note: *This delicious dough is very fragile and is difficult to roll and cut without breaking. If you want to try to cut individual heart-shaped cookies, try rolling the dough directly onto a piece of parchment and chilling again before you cut the heart shapes. Then, after you cut the entire sheet of hearts, gently peel away the excess dough and work it into other shapes for baking.*

This rhyme goes back to the late 1700's. But it became famous in the work of Lewis G. Carroll in 'Alice in Wonderland', published in 1805.

The Queen of Hearts

The Queen of Hearts she made some tarts all on
a summer's day;
The Knave of Hearts he stole the tarts and took
them clean away.
The King of Hearts called for the tarts and beat
the Knave full sore.
The Knave of Hearts brought back the tarts and
vowed he'd steal no more.

Gingerbread People

Makes approximately 36 small cookies

This recipe for gingerbread cookies is used in Blackbird Pie.

INGREDIENTS:

- 4 cups white whole wheat flour
- 3/4 teaspoon baking soda
- 2/3 cup dark brown sugar, packed
- 1 teaspoon salt
- 3/4 cup butter
- 3 large eggs
- 2/3 cup molasses
- 4 teaspoons ground ginger
- 1 teaspoon ground cloves
- 1 tablespoon ground cinnamon
- 1/2 teaspoon ground mace

DIRECTIONS:

In a medium bowl, sift together flour, baking soda, salt and spices. Set aside.

In a large bowl, cream the butter until it is light and fluffy. Add the sugar and mix again until light and creamy. Blend in the eggs one at a time and then the molasses. Add the flour mixture in two additions either by hand or on low speed. Wrap dough in plastic and chill.

Heat oven to 350 ° F. Line the baking sheet with parchment paper.

Roll the dough out onto a lightly floured surface, roughly 1/8 inch thick. Cut into gingerbread men (or other desired shapes). Transfer to baking sheets and bake for 7–10 minutes.

Gingerbread Man

Run, run, run as fast as you can.
You'll never catch me, I'm the gingerbread man.

Almost Too Much Ginger Cookies

Makes 12 – 16 cookies

INGREDIENTS:

- 1 1/2 tablespoons grated fresh ginger root
- 1 cup sugar
- 1/2 cup butter
- 1/4 cup buttermilk
- 1 egg
- 1/4 cup honey
- 1/2 cup crystallized ginger, finely chopped (Below)
- 2 cups all-purpose flour
- 2 teaspoons ground ginger
- 2 teaspoons baking soda
- 1/2 teaspoon salt

DIRECTIONS:

Peel the fresh ginger and grate it into the cup of sugar. Stir it together and allow it to sit, refrigerated, overnight or for at least 2 hours. In a large bowl, cream together the butter until soft. Add sugar and grated, fresh ginger mixture and beat until smooth. Gradually beat in the egg, buttermilk and honey. Add flour, ground ginger, baking soda, salt and crystallized ginger. Cover and refrigerate dough for at least 2 hours.

BAKING:

Preheat oven to 350 ° F. Shape dough into balls about the size of golf balls and flatten on un-greased cookie sheet. A sheet of baking parchment can make the cookies brown better without burning or sticking. Bake 10 minutes or until lightly browned. Cool on wire racks.

Homemade Crystallized Ginger

Scrape the peeling from a piece of fresh ginger root with the edge of a small spoon. Slice into 1/8" pieces. Simmer slowly for 2 hours in ¼ water and 2 cups sugar.

Cool to lukewarm and then roll the cooked ginger slices in sugar and store in an airtight container.

Marmalade Cookies

Makes about 24 – 30 cookies

INGREDIENTS:

- 2/3 cup sugar
- 1/3 cup butter
- 1 egg
- 6 tablespoons orange or other citrus marmalade
- 1 ½ cups all-purpose flour
- 1 ½ baking powder
- Baking parchment (optional)

DIRECTIONS:

Preheat oven to 375°F. Grease the baking sheet or cover with a sheet of baking parchment.

Cream together the butter and sugar. Mix in the egg until creamy. Add the marmalade.

Sift together the flour and baking powder. Stir into the butter mixture.

Refrigerate the cookie dough for at least 30 minutes. Bake a test cookie. If the cookie is too dry, add another tablespoon of marmalade. If it is too moist, add a tablespoon of flour.

Bake the remaining cookies.

Cool and serve.

Cookies may keep fresh a bit longer if stored in a tightly closed container.

NOTE:

Another jam or flavor of preserve can be substituted for marmalade. Strawberry jam and fig jam work well – as long as it is a thick, pulpy preserve and not a jelly.

Chocolate Cracker Cookies

Makes about 24 – 30 cookies

INGREDIENTS:

- 2/3 cup semi-sweet chocolate chips
- 2 egg whites
- ½ teaspoon vanilla
- ¼ teaspoon cream of tartar
- 2/3 cup sugar
- ½ cup crushed graham crackers
- Baking parchment (optional)

DIRECTIONS:

Preheat oven to 350°F. Grease the baking sheet or cover with a sheet of baking parchment.

Place the chocolate chips in a heat-proof mixing bowl. Set the bowl in water that is hot enough to melt the chocolate chips or let the bowl sit on a saucepan filled with water at a low simmer – until the chocolate melts. Let cool for 10 minutes.

Beat the egg whites until stiff. Add the vanilla and cream of tartar. Gradually beat in the sugar. Gently fold in the crushed cracker crumbs and the melted, cooled chocolate.

Drop the mixture by spoonfuls onto the prepared baking sheet. Bake 10 – 12 minutes until the cookie is puffed into a dome shape.

Cool and serve.

Cookies may keep fresh a bit longer if stored in a tightly closed container.

Fresh Fruit Fun

Strawberry Flowers
Apple Flowers
Flower Fruit Salad with Crystallized Violets
Berry Bread Salad
Tea-Poached Pears
Orange Cups
Baked Apple Rings
Stuffed Baked apples
Un-Baked Banana Boats
Baked Banana Boats

Strawberry Flowers

Makes 4 servings

INGREDIENTS:

- 4 tablespoons cream cheese
- 2 teaspoons honey
- 12 large ripe, un-bruised strawberries
- 12 large fresh blueberries
- 1/4 cup yogurt
- 12 sprigs of fresh mint leaves

DIRECTIONS:

Wash the strawberries and blueberries. Let them dry on paper towels.

Soften the cream cheese and honey and stir together until smooth and creamy. Form the cream cheese into 12 small balls to secure the cut strawberries to a plate and to hold the leaves in place. Put three cheese balls on each plate, about 1 1/2 inches apart.

Place the large end of each of the strawberries into one of the cream cheese balls. Cut the strawberries into wedges but do not cut them all the way through. Fold the cut strawberry "petals" out far enough to insert a small dollop of yogurt and one of the whole blueberries.

Decorate with small sprigs of mint leaves under each strawberry by sticking the stem into the cream cheese.

If you're not going to serve immediately, then the fruit flowers should be covered and refrigerated.

Apple Flowers

INGREDIENTS:

- Apples, 1 per person

And an assortment of optional decorations:

- Yogurt – your favorite flavors
- Raisins
- Dried cranberries
- Lemon curd
- Almond slivers
- Sunflower seeds
- Mandarin orange slices
- Pomegranate pieces
- Flaked coconut
- Whipped cream
- Raspberry sauce or other fruit flavored syrup

DIRECTIONS:

Serve one small apple flower per person or share an apple between two people.

Just before serving, wash and core each apple. Cut the apple into eight equal wedges. For larger apples, you might cut more wedges. The cut wedges can be kept from turning brown by sprinkling them with lemon juice.

Arrange the wedges on the plate in a circle, like an open flower where each wedge is a petal. At the center of the circle, spoon a dipping sauce of your choice. This can be yogurt, clotted cream, whipped cream, lemon curd or you can decorate the flower with dribbled raspberry sauce, sunflower seeds or coconut.

AS A PARTY ACTIVITY:

Provide the toppings and edible decorations and children can create their own apple flowers.

Flower Fruit Salad

Serves 4 – 6

INGREDIENTS:

Crystallized Flowers:

- 1 cup violets or Johnny-Jump-Ups
- 1 cup superfine sugar
- ½ teaspoon warm water
- 1 egg white
- Baking parchment

The Fresh Salad:

- 1 cup edible flower petals: Rose Petals, Carnation Petals**
- 4 cups sliced or cubed fresh fruit: a combination of strawberries, blueberries, grapes, melon, bananas, oranges or other seasonal favorites
- Fresh mint leaves, finely chopped

*** Flower petals can be all one kind of flower or a combination of edible blossoms and herbs: roses, day lilies, violets, calendula and mint are a few suggestions.*

DIRECTIONS:

Crystallizing Violets – Make the day ahead!

Preheat oven to 200 ° F.

Wash the violets or Johnny-Jump-Ups thoroughly and allow them to dry on paper towel. Whip the egg white and ½ teaspoon warm water until frothy. Dip the flowers into the egg white and then into the sugar. Place them on a baking sheet lined with parchment. Let dry in the 200 ° oven for 1 hour with the oven door slightly open. Turn off the oven, close the door and allow the heat of the oven to continue drying.

Making The Salad

Trim the flower petals away from the stems, wash thoroughly and dry. Cut the fruit and combine with flowers. Decorate the top with crystallized violets. As a salad, this can be served without a dressing –a sweet dressing, yogurt or juice.

Berry Bread Salad

Serves 6 – 8

This is a wonderful summertime recipe when wild berries are ripe
and many berries are in season in your local market.

INGREDIENTS:

- 1/4 cup butter
- 1/4 cup brown sugar
- 1 teaspoon ground cinnamon
- 2 cups bread cubes
- 3 cup your choice of berries; strawberries, blueberries, raspberries, blackberries, or all one kind of berry
- 1–2 cups sweet, berry-flavored yogurt

DIRECTIONS:

Preheat oven to 350 ° F.

Melt the butter in a large skillet (one that can be transferred to the oven) over low heat. Stir in 1/4 cup of the sugar and all the cinnamon until the sugar and cinnamon dissolve. Remove from the stove. Add bread cubes and stir them so that the hot mixture coats a bit of each piece of bread. Pour the bread cubes out into a lasagna roasting pan and spread them out thinly.

Put the pan in the oven for 10 – 15 minutes or until bread is toasted. Remove the pan two times during the baking to stir them.

While the bread is in the oven, place 1 cup of the berries in a small bowl and mash them with the remaining 1/4 cup of brown sugar. They should be pulpy and very juicy.

When the bread is toasted, transfer it to a large serving bowl and let it cool for 5 minutes. Add the whole berries and mix well. Finally, add the mashed berries and toss together. Chill for a few minutes before serving. Add a spoonful of yogurt to the top of each serving of salad.

Tea Poached Pears

Serves 4

INGREDIENTS:

- 6 fruit flavored tea bags
- 3 cups water
- 1/2 cup honey
- 2 whole pears, peeled, cored and halved
- 1 cup vanilla flavored yogurt

DIRECTIONS:

Heat water in a wide bottomed saucepan. When water is lightly simmering, turn off heat and add teabags. Cover to steep 5 – 10 minutes. Remove teabags and add honey. Stir until honey is completely dissolved. Bring the tea back to a gentle simmer and allow to reduce while you peel and core the pears. Place pears into the pan. Cover and poach for 8 minutes. The pears will float in the tea but you should turn them over in the liquid during poaching until they're soft. You should be able to pierce them with a fork. Cook to your desired softness.

Chill the pears before serving. A bed of shredded lettuce will support the pear. Fill the scooped-out portion of the pear with a spoonful of yogurt.

Pears can be poached the day before your tea. And you can substitute own favorite flavor yogurt for the vanilla. This can be garnished with mint leaves, fresh fruit slices or edible flowers.

Orange Cups

Makes 4 servings

INGREDIENTS:

- 2 navel oranges
- 24 grapes
- 1 cup dried, sweetened cranberries or fruit combination of your choice
- 1 cup lemon flavored yogurt

DIRECTIONS:

With a sharp paring knife, cut orange in half. Carefully remove the orange pulp with a small paring knife and carve orange into small bites. Mix fruit and fill the orange "bowls". Top with spoonful of yogurt.

Note: *To keep the orange bowl steady, trim the bottom to make it level.*

Oranges and Lemons

Say the bells of St Clement's.
You owe me five farthings
Say the bells of St Martin's.
When will you pay me?
Say the bells of Old Bailey.
When I grow rich
Say the bells of Shoreditch.
When will that be?
Say the bells of Stepney.
I do not know
Says the great bell at Bow.

Baked Apple Rings
Serves 6

INGREDIENTS:

- 1 cup sugar
- ½ cup water
- 3 apples

DIRECTIONS:

Preheat oven to 325°F.

Place sugar and water in a saucepan. Simmer over medium-high heat until the sugar begins to caramelize and the water evaporates, 8 – 10 minutes. Stir gently and watch so that it does not burn.

Remove from heat immediately when it reaches the brown caramel color and pour it into a flat baking dish. Allow it to cool while you prepare the apple rings.

Core the whole apples, removing the stem and seeds but leaving the peel. Trim the top and bottom ends from the apple to expose the white apple. Then cut the remaining apple in half. Place the apple rings in the caramel-lined baking dish.

Bake the apple rings for 20 – 25 minutes, until they are soft. Remove the apples from the pan quickly while the caramel is still soft, lifting them out carefully so that you are not burned. Invert the apple rings onto the serving plate. Serve the rings with the caramel side up. Be careful to let them cool slightly before serving. Top with ice cream or whipped cream, if desired.

Stuffed Baked Apples

Serves 4

INGREDIENTS:

- 4 large baking apples
- ½ cup dried cranberries or raisins
- 1/4 cup brown sugar
- 2 tablespoons butter
- 1 teaspoon cinnamon
- 1/2 cup granola
- 1/4 cup chopped pecans or walnuts (optional)
- 1 cup warm water

DIRECTIONS:

Preheat oven to 375 ° F.

Wash apples. Remove most of the core, starting with the stem. Do not cut all the way to the bottom. You can use a paring knife or a special apple-coring tool. Widen the hole for stuffing.

In a small bowl, combine the sugar, cinnamon, cranberries or raisins, and pecans. Place apples in a baking pan. Stuff each apple with this mixture. Top with a dot of butter.

Add the warm water to the baking pan. Bake 30 minutes or until tender, but not mushy. Baste the apples with the pan juices several times during cooking. They are done when the apples can be pierced easily with a fork. Remove from oven and cool slightly before serving.

Serve as is or with:

Homemade Whipped Cream, page 128

Mock Devonshire Cream page 129 or

Butterscotch Sauce, page 133.

Un-Baked Banana Boats

Serves 4

INGREDIENTS:

- 4 bananas
- 1 cup peanut butter (either smooth or crunchy)
- 1/4 cup honey

Decoration Suggestions:

- Fruit leather
- Kabob skewers
- Miniature marshmallows
- Raisins or dried cranberries
- Chocolate Chips
- Shredded coconut

DIRECTIONS:

Peel the bananas and "glue" them to the plate with a small spoonful of peanut butter. Stabilize it as needed with some of the edible decorations. Marshmallows and chocolate chips can help support the banana and keep it from falling over. Mix the honey and peanut butter. Cut away a 'V' shaped trough in the banana, being careful not to cut to the end. Fill with the peanut butter and honey mixture.

ACTIVITY:

Each child can decorate his/her Banana Boat with the various choices. A piece of fruit leather can be a sail strung on the kabob skewer.

Row, Row, Row Your Boat

Row, row, row your boat,
Gently down the stream,
Merrily, merrily, merrily, merrily,
Life is but a dream.

Baked Banana Boats

INGREDIENTS:

- 1 banana per person
- Miniature marshmallows
- Chocolate chips
- Baking parchment

DIRECTIONS:

Preheat oven to 350 ° F.

On a sheet of baking parchment, place banana with its peel on. Slice the peeled banana lengthwise, but don't cut completely through. Squeeze apart slightly. Sprinkle chocolate chips and then marshmallows in opening of banana. Bring parchment up loosely and fold it closed on top and ends. Place in oven for 15 minutes. To serve, remove paper and add a decorative paper sail. Banana can be eaten out of peel with a spoon.

ACTIVITY:

Children can decorate a triangular sail while they wait for their banana to bake.

Excerpt from:

Wynken, Blynken, and Nod (1889)

by Eugene Field

Wynken, Blynken, and Nod one night
Sailed off in a wooden shoe—
Sailed on a river of crystal light,
Into a sea of dew.
"Where are you going, and what do you wish?"
The old moon asked the three.
"We have come to fish for the herring fish
That live in this beautiful sea;
Nets of silver and gold have we!"
Said Wynken, Blynken, And Nod.

Special Sandwiches

Snowflake Cinnamon Toast
Open-Faced Strawberry Sandwiches
Triple Butter Sandwiches & Apple Butter
Nutty-Fruity Sandwich Spread
Carrt-Nut Sandwich Spread
Apple Chicken Spread
Turkey In The Straw
Apple, Ham & Cheese Stuffed-wiches
Funny Face-wiches
Choco-Nut Sandwich Spread

Snowflake Cinnamon Toast

Serves 4

This is usually a breakfast recipe but is fun for lunch or afternoon tea.

INGREDIENTS:

- 4 pieces of bread
- 1 stick of butter, melted (or 1/2 cup butter substitute, melted)
- 1 cup granulated sugar
- 2 tablespoons ground cinnamon
- 1/2 cup powdered sugar
- A Snowflake stencil — or other decoration of your choice
- 2 cups applesauce

DIRECTIONS:

Preheat the broiler.

Blend the cinnamon and sugar. Melt the butter. Place the bread on a flat baking sheet. It helps prevent burning and makes clean-up easier to line the baking pan with parchment. With a pastry brush, coat one side of the bread with the melted butter. Broil until very lightly browned. Remove from the broiler and turn the bread.

Warm the applesauce while the bread is cooking.

Coat the other side with melted butter.

Sprinkle the surface of the bread with a generous coating of the cinnamon-sugar mixture. Return to the broiler but watch carefully. The sugar will melt into the butter and bubble, forming a crusty sugar topping for the cinnamon toast. While the toast is cooking, add powdered sugar to a sifter. Remove toast from the oven and lay the stencil(s) on top of each piece. Then dust with powdered sugar while the toast is still warm. Serve with warm applesauce.

ACTIVITY:

Cutting paper snowflakes has been a traditional winter craft for generations. An older child can make his/her own snowflake decoration by folding and cutting the paper. A younger child will need assistance.

Open-Faced Strawberry Sandwiches
Makes 4 – 6 servings

INGREDIENTS:

- 2 baskets fresh strawberries
- 2 tablespoons lemon juice
- 2 tablespoons powdered sugar
- 1 cup heavy whipping cream
- 6–8 oz. cream cheese, softened and spreadable
- 6 slices a sweet bread: possibly Lemon Angel Bread or Fairy Flower Bread, pages 80 – 82

DIRECTIONS:

Preheat oven to 325 ° F.

Choose the largest and most ripe strawberries for slicing. Slice half of the strawberries. Mash the other half and add lemon juice. Whip the cream. Add powdered sugar at the soft peak stage. Lightly toast the slices of bread and spread with cream cheese. Top with strawberries and a dollop of whipped cream. Serve immediately.

Curly Locks

Curly Locks, Curly Locks, Will you be mine?
You shall not wash dishes, Nor feed the swine,
But sit on a cushion And sew a fine seam,
And sup upon strawberries, Sugar, and cream.

Triple Butter Sandwiches

Makes 4 sandwiches

We introduced this recipe in "Emma Lea's Tea With Daddy".

INGREDIENTS:

- 1/4 cup honey
- 1/2 cup butter
- 1/2 cup almond butter or peanut butter
- 1/2 cup apple butter

DIRECTIONS:

Into softened butter, mix the honey until smooth and spreadable. Spread one piece of bread with honey butter and the other slice of bread with almond butter. Spread apple butter in between and close the sandwich.

This filling is especially good on the Cinnamon Spiral Bread page 98.

NOTE:

Some health food stores have a nut grinder to make almond butter from almonds and peanuts. It seems to make a trip to the market an extra-special treat for young children.

Homemade Apple Butter

INGREDIENTS:

- 2 pounds fresh apples
- 1 cup sugar
- 3/4 cup water
- 1 teaspoon cinnamon
- 1/2 teaspoon cloves

DIRECTIONS:

Peel, core and cut up the apples. Combine with the water and cook over very low heat until the apples are soft. Add sugar and spices. Continue to cook over low heat, mashing cooked apple pieces as they soften and stirring frequently, until the mixture becomes a thick pulp. Store in the refrigerator for 1 week. Freeze or can any that will not be used quickly.

Nutty-Fruity Sandwich Spread

Makes 3 – 4 sandwiches

INGREDIENTS:

- 1 cup cream cheese, softened
- 1/4 cup frozen orange juice
- 1/2 cup pecans or walnuts
- 1 cup dried cranberries

DIRECTIONS:

Beat the cream cheese with orange juice concentrate until smooth. Chop the nuts and cranberries together and add to the cream cheese.

Spread on sandwich bread at room temperature.

Try this spread on our Lemon Angel Bread, page 80 or on the Cinnamon Spiral Bread, page 98.

Note: *Chopping the nuts and cranberries together makes the cranberries less sticky and a bit easier to chop quickly.*

Your Notes

Carrot-Nut Sandwich Spread

Makes 4 sandwiches

INGREDIENTS:

- 1 8-oz. package cream cheese
- 1 tablespoon lemon juice
- 1 cup finely grated carrot
- 1/4 cup unsalted sunflower seeds
- 1/4 cup white raisins
- 1/4 cup dried, sweetened cranberries

DIRECTIONS:

Soften the cream cheese by stirring in the lemon juice with a fork until creamy. Add other ingredients to the cream cheese mixture. It should form a spread-able paste. It is easier to spread at room temperature, just after you've mixed it. But it should be covered and refrigerated if not being used immediately.

Recommended bread recipes for tea sandwiches:

Crumpet, page 100

Sweet Popovers, page 87.

Do You Carrot All For Me

Anonymous

Do you carrot all for me? My heart beets for you,
With your turnip nose and your radish face,
You are a peach.
If we cantaloupe, lettuce marry:
Weed make a swell pear.

Apple Chicken Salad
Makes 4 – 6 servings

INGREDIENTS:

- 2 cups cooked, diced chicken
- 2 cups diced apple
- 1/2 cup diced celery
- 1/2 cup dried cranberries
- 1/2 cup mayonnaise
- 3 oz. package cream cheese
- 1/4 cup lemon juice
- 1/2 teaspoon salt

DIRECTIONS:

Soften the cream cheese. Add in the mayonnaise, lemon juice and salt. Stir until creamy.

Chop the cooked chicken very fine. The apples and celery should also be cut into finely diced pieces. Add the chicken, apple, celery and cranberries to the cheese and mayonnaise mixture. Refrigerate for 1 hour or overnight to let the flavors meld. Stir the mixture well to soften before spreading it on a sandwich.

This filling is good on the Lemon Angel Bread, page 80.

But it is also fun to serve open-faced on a toasted Crumpet, page 100.

Turkey In The Straw
Serves 4

INGREDIENTS:

- 2 cups cooked turkey, chopped
- 4 ounces cream cheese (1/2 an 8-oz. package)
- 1 small red bell pepper, chopped
- 1/2 cup grated Monterey Jack cheese
- 2 green onions, finely chopped
- Salt, to taste
- 2 tablespoons parsley, finely chopped
- 2 cups dry chow mein noodles
- 1 tablespoon light vegetable oil
- Toasted Crumpets, page 100 or on commercial English Muffin
- 2 tablespoons black olives, chopped

DIRECTIONS:

Preheat oven to 450 ° F.

Soften the cream cheese in the bowl and stir in turkey, bell pepper, cheese, onion, salt and parsley. This should form a mixture that is loose but sticky.

Build a nest with the noodles on top of a Crumpet or English Muffin. Fill with a spoonful of the turkey and cheese mixture. Bake until the cheese on top melts and begins to brown. Serve immediately.

The folk tune, "Turkey In The Straw" became popular in the early 1800s and has inspired many versions and verses. This is one common refrain.

Turkey In the Straw

Turkey in the hay, in the hay, in the hay.
Turkey in the straw, in straw, in the straw,
Pick up your fiddle and rosin your bow,
And put on a tune called Turkey in the straw.

Apple, Ham & Cheese Stuffed-wiches

Serves 4 – 6

The surprise ingredient of the apple makes it a bit more fun for children. But this recipe can be made with ham and cheese alone in a more traditional mode.

INGREDIENTS:

- 1 loaf brown-n-serve bread or half-baked bread from your bakery
- 1 cup finely chopped apple
- 2 cups chopped ham
- 1 cup grated cheddar cheese
- 1 - 8 oz. package cream cheese
- 2 eggs, beaten

DIRECTIONS:

Preheat oven to 450 ° F.

Cut ends off the loaf of bread with a sharp knife, cut out the center of the loaf of bread, leaving a tube.

Soften the cream cheese and stir in the beaten egg to form a paste. Mix in all the other ingredients and stuff them into the loaf of bread. Replace the ends of the bread loaf and secure with toothpicks. Count the number of toothpicks used. Bake the loaf for about 25 minutes, until the loaf is golden brown and crispy on the outside and the inside cheese is melted.

Remove the toothpicks. Make sure you count and do not leave a toothpick. Allow the loaf to cool for about 5 minutes before slicing the rounds. Serve immediately.

Note: *Create your own stuffed sandwich recipes with your favorite ingredients. This works with everything from chicken salad to meatballs. Let your imagination be your guide.*

Funny Face-wiches

Serves 4

This is an activity recipe.
It can also become a spontaneous rainy day lunch and generate an
hour of giggles and memories to share with your young child.

INGREDIENTS:

- Crumpets or English Muffins
- Peanut Butter or Almond Butter
- Cream Cheese – can be colored or flavored
- Raisins
- Full Sheet fruit leather or roll-ups
- Gummy candies
- Hazelnuts (make a great nose)
- Other fun things from your cupboard!

DIRECTIONS:

Prepare the sample face and have the topping choices for each child.

Toast the bread lightly and serve to each child.

Assist younger children in spreading the nut butter on their muffin.

Then decorate and eat.

Can be a seasonal or themed menu item.

Like Face-Witches – create a black-hat and ugly features

Choco-Nut Sandwich Spread

Serves 4 – 6

INGREDIENTS:

- 1 8-oz package cream cheese
- 1/2 cup semi-sweet chocolate chips, melted
- 1 teaspoon almond extract
- 2 tablespoons powdered sugar
- ½ cup chopped pecans or almonds
- ¼ cup shredded coconut

DIRECTIONS:

Set the cream cheese out at room temperature to soften.

Place the chocolate chips into a heat-proof mixing bowl. Set over a pan of boiling water until the chocolate is melted. Cool for 10 minutes. Stir in the cream cheese, vanilla and powdered sugar. Blend well.

Stir in the nuts and coconut. Keep at room temperature for easy spreading or cover and refrigerate if you are not serving immediately.

Good as a sandwich spread on open-faced Crumpets, page 100

Cinnamon Spiral Bread, page 98

or Lemon Angel Bread, page 80.

Crepes

Tunnles of Love
Apple Pie Roll-ups
Lemon-Cheese Crepes
Vegetable Roll-Ups

Tunnels of Love

Makes 8 Crepes

This recipe was included in "Emma Lea's Magic Teapot".

INGREDIENTS:

Crepe Batter:

- 1 cup flour
- 1 teaspoon baking powder
- 1 pinch salt
- 2 tablespoons powdered sugar
- 1 egg
- 1 cup milk
- 1/2 teaspoon vanilla
- Vegetable oil

Filling:

- 3–4 bananas
- 16–20 strawberries

Apricot Sauce:

- 1 cup of apricot jam
- 1/2 cup water

DIRECTIONS:

To Prepare Batter:

Sift together the flour, baking powder, salt and powdered sugar. Beat the egg and add milk and vanilla. Blend milk and egg mixture into flour.

Let sit, covered, for a minimum of 30 minutes before cooking the crepes. This can be in the refrigerator or at room temperature if it is not too hot.

To Cook Crepes:

Heat small skillet over a moderate flame and add a few drops of vegetable oil to the pan for each crepe. Ladle a small quantity of the thin batter into the pan and shake or tip the pan to have it cover the entire bottom of the pan.

Cook each crepe quickly over moderate heat. Allow it to lightly brown on one side. Lift it gently with a fork or spatula and flip to cook the other side.

Crepes can be cooked prior to filling and set aside. If they are not overcooked, they will remain soft and can be rolled with the filling.

Prepare Filling:

Slice bananas into 1/2 inch round slices. Chop strawberries into small pieces. On top of each open crepe, create a row of banana rounds with spaces for the chopped strawberries.

Prepare Apricot Sauce:

Combine apricot jam and water in a small saucepan. Heat until the jam melts and is completely blended with the water. Simmer 5 minutes, stirring occasionally.

Finishing the Tunnels of Love:

Pour a light covering of the apricot sauce over the top of the crepes. Heat the oven to 450 º F. Warm them in the oven until the apricot sauce begins to simmer. Serve immediately.

Note:

Crepes can also be cooked, filled and served immediately in most recipes. This is specifically written so that a child can help assemble the 'tunnels' and then the entire pan is baked for a short time to reheat the crepes and the topping.

Apple Pie Roll-Ups

Make 6 – 8 crepes

This is easier than pie!

INGREDIENTS:

Crepe Batter:

- 1 egg, beaten
- 1 cup milk
- 1 cup flour
- 1 pinch salt
- 1 teaspoon baking powder
- 1 tablespoon powdered sugar
- 1/2 teaspoon vanilla
- Light vegetable oil

Filling:

- 4 tart apples — peeled, cored and thinly sliced
- 1 tablespoon light oil
- 1/4 cup brown sugar
- 2 tablespoon flour
- 1 teaspoon cinnamon
- 1 tablespoon lemon juice
- 1 cup water

Apricot Glaze:

- 1 cup apricot jam
- 1/2 cup water

DIRECTIONS:

Crepe Batter:

Whisk together all ingredients, except the oil, and let sit for at least 30 minutes in the refrigerator before cooking. Use small amounts of oil in the pan to cook crepes over moderate heat. Ladle thin batter into hot pan and cook each side for about 2 minutes – until there is some light browning. Cook the entire batch or as many as you need. Cool before assembling.

Filling:

Heat oil in a skillet and sauté apple slices until soft. Sprinkle with brown sugar and cinnamon until sugar is melted. Sprinkle lightly with flour and stir gently until flour is completely moistened. Add lemon juice and water. Mix and simmer until sauce thickens and apples are soft.

Apricot Glaze:

Heat 1 cup apricot jam with 1/2 cup water. Mix well as jam melts.

Assembly:

Preheat oven to 425 ° F.

Fill crepes with apple filling and roll into a tube. Save apple slices, 1 per crepe — for decorative topping. Drizzle with glaze and decorate with an apple slice.

Bake until just warm — about 10 minutes — when the glaze begins to bubble. Serve while warm.

If all the world was apple-pie
And all the sea was ink;
And all the trees were bread and cheese,
What would we do for drink?

Lemon-Cheese Crepes

Makes 8 Crepes

INGREDIENTS:

Crepe Batter:

- 1 cup flour
- 1 teaspoon baking powder
- 1 pinch salt
- 2 tablespoons powdered sugar
- 1 egg
- 1 cup milk
- ½ teaspoon vanilla
- Vegetable oil

Filling:

- 2 cups ricotta cheese
- 2 eggs
- 1 recipe Lemon Curd, page 129

Apricot Sauce:

- 1 cup apricot jam
- ½ cup water

DIRECTIONS:

Sift together the flour, baking powder, salt and powdered sugar. Beat the egg and add milk and vanilla. Blend milk and egg mixture into flour and let set for 30 minutes.

To Cook Crepes:

Heat small skillet and add a few drops of vegetable oil to the pan for each crepe. Ladle a small quantity of the thin batter into the pan and shake or tip the pan to have it cover the entire surface of the pan.

Cook each crepe quickly over moderate heat. Allow it to lightly brown on one side. Lift it gently with a fork or spatula and flip to cook the other side.

Crepes can be cooked prior to filling and set aside. If they are not overcooked, they will remain soft and can be rolled with the filling.

Filling:

Beat the eggs well. Stir in the ricotta cheese. It helps to chill the filling for 30 minutes before trying to assemble the crepes. To fill the crepe, spoon some of the cheese filling and lemon curd into each open crepe, close to one edge. Roll it into a tube and place in a greased baking dish with the flap side down. Leave 1/4" between the crepes while baking.

Apricot Sauce:

Heat together until well blended.

Finishing the Crepes

Preheat the oven to 450 °F.

Pour a light covering of the apricot sauce over the top of the crepes. Bake them until the apricot sauce begins to simmer. Serve immediately.

Your Notes

Vegetable Roll-Ups

Makes 8 Crepes

INGREDIENTS:

Crepe Batter:

- 1 cup flour
- 1 teaspoon baking powder
- 1 pinch salt
- 1 egg
- 1 cup milk
- Vegetable oil

Filling:

- 2 cups ricotta cheese
- 2 eggs
- 1 onion, diced
- 2 cloves garlic, minced
- 2 zucchini, diced
- 1 red bell pepper, diced
- 6 mushrooms, chopped

Béchamel Sauce:

- 1/4 cup butter
- 1/4 cup all-purpose flour
- 2 cups milk
- Salt and white pepper to taste
- Nutmeg, just a pinch

DIRECTIONS:

To Make the Crepe Batter:

Sift together the flour, baking powder and salt. Beat the egg and add milk. Blend milk and egg mixture into flour and let set for 30 minutes.

To Cook Crepes:

Heat small skillet and add a few drops of vegetable oil to the pan for each crepe. Ladle a small quantity of the thin batter into the pan and shake or tip the pan to have it cover the entire surface of the pan. Crepe should be extremely thin – not like a pancake. Cook each crepe quickly over moderate heat. Allow it to lightly brown on one side. Lift it gently with a fork or spatula and flip to cook the other side. Crepes can be cooked prior to filling and set aside. If they are not overcooked, they will remain soft and can be rolled with the filling. They can be stored for a short time with waxed paper separations so they don't stick together.

Prepare the filling:

Beat the eggs well. Stir in the ricotta cheese. It helps to chill the filling for 30 minutes before trying to assemble the crepes. Sauté the onion and garlic until the onion becomes translucent. Add zucchini, bell pepper and mushrooms. Continue to cook until the vegetables are tender but not too soft. Remove from heat.

Fill the crepes:

To fill the crepe, spoon some of the cheese filling and vegetable mixture into each open crepe, close to one edge. Roll it into a tube and place in a greased baking dish with the flap side down. Leave 1/4" between the crepes while baking.

Béchamel Sauce:

In a medium heavy saucepan, melt butter over low heat. When butter starts to foam, add the flour all at once, mixing well with a wooden spoon. Cook over low heat 3 to 4 minutes, stirring constantly to incorporate and cook flour. Remove pan from heat.

Finishing the Crepes

Preheat the oven to 450 °F.

Pour a light covering of the Béchamel Sauce over the top of the crepes. Bake them until the sauce begins to simmer. Serve immediately.

Quick & Easy Breads

Pat-A-Cakes
Lemon Angel Bread
Fairy Flower Bread & Crystallized Violets
Blueberry-Orange Scones
Chunky Apple Scones
Mandarin Orange Scones
Applesauce Muffins
Pumpkin Spice Bread
Sweet Popovers
Corny Bread Muffins
Vegetable Sandwich Bread
Cheese Crusts
Homemade Crackers

Pat-A-Cakes

Makes 8 cakes

INGREDIENTS:

- 1 1/2 cups all-purpose flour
- 1/3 cup sugar
- 2 teaspoons baking powder
- 1/2 teaspoon salt
- 3/4 cup whipping cream
- 2 teaspoons finely grated lemon peel
- 1 cup black or golden raisins

DIRECTIONS:

Preheat oven to 375 ° F.

Grease a baking sheet.

In a large mixing bowl combine the flour, the sugar, \baking powder and salt. Make a big dent or well in the center of flour mixture. Add whipping cream and lemon peel.

Stir until mixture is crumbly. Coat hands with a little flour. Use your hands to gently knead the dough in the mixing bowl until it can be formed into a ball. Turn dough out onto a lightly floured surface.

Gently roll or pat the dough into a 7-1/2-inch circle. Using a table knife, cut the dough like a pizza into 8 wedges. Do not separate the wedges. Shift the dough onto the greased baking sheet.

"Mark" each wedge with the initial of one guest by pressing the raisins into the surface in the shape of the letter. Bake for 12 minutes or until golden.

Pat-A-Cake

Pat a cake, Pat a cake, baker's man
Bake me a cake as fast as you can;
Pat it and prick it and mark it with a 'B',
And put it in the oven for Baby and me.

The exact origins of the Pat a Cake poem are not known but it may go back to the 1600's. And the tradition of decorating a cake with the name or initial of the person with the birthday have been common for centuries.

The way this rhyme song is performed is with clapping. But a variation can be enjoyed as a group activity by substituting the first letter of the guest's name at the end of the third line and then that name in the fourth.

All children past and present enjoy this traditional song. This traditional song of the ages goes back in time and will likely go long into the future.

Lemon Angel Bread

Makes 1 large loaf

This bread is light, like Angel Food Cake but not sweet.

INGREDIENTS:

- 1 cups cake flour
- 1/2 teaspoon salt
- 8 egg whites, chilled
- Finely grated peeling from one lemon
- 1 ½ teaspoon cream of tartar
- 1/2 cup sugar
- 1 tablespoon lemon juice

DIRECTIONS:

Preheat oven to 350 ºF.

Grate the lemon peel and squeeze the juice. Sift flour before measuring. Then sift together flour and sugar. Set aside. Beat the chilled egg whites until foamy and starting to peak. Then add salt and cream of tartar. Continue beating until the peaks are stiff. Add lemon peel and lemon juice. Using a spatula, slowly fold the dry ingredients into the egg whites. This process should take 5 – 7 minutes. Transfer to an un-greased bread pan and bake until the top is browned and it bounces back when touched, about 30 minutes. Do not attempt to slice the bread until it is completely cool.

Sandwich Suggestion: Serve open-faced with Strawberries & Cream Filling, page 57 or make a complete sandwich with Cranberry-Pecan Spread page 59.

Come up here, O dusty feet! Here is fairy bread to eat.
Here in my retiring room, Children, you may dine
On the golden smell of broom, and the shade of pine;
And when you have eaten well, Fairy stories hear and tell.

Robert Louis Stevenson

Fairy Flower Bread

Makes 24

INGREDIENTS:

- 1 recipe for Lemon Angel Bread, page 80
- 2 cups fresh flower petals

Flower petals can be all one kind of flower or a combination of edible blossoms and herbs: roses, day lilies, violets, calendula and mint are a few suggestions.

DIRECTIONS:

Separate the flower petals. Break into small pieces. Wash in cold water. Strain and allow to dry completely on a clean towel. Chop lightly. Set aside.

Prepare the recipe for Angel Bread. Fold the flower petals into the batter just before baking.

Optional: Prepare a recipe of the Crystallized Violets and decorate the surface of the bread before serving

Crystallized Violets

INGREDIENTS:

- 1 cup Violets or Johnny-Jump-Ups
- 1 cup superfine sugar
- ½ teaspoon warm water
- 1 egg white
- Baking parchment

DIRECTIONS:

Preheat oven to 200 ° F.

Wash the violets or Johnny-Jump-Ups thoroughly and allow them to dry on paper towel. Whip the egg white and ½ teaspoon warm water until frothy. Dip the flowers into the egg white and then into the sugar. Place them on a baking sheet lined with parchment. Let dry in the 200 ° oven for 1 hour with the oven door slightly open. Turn off the oven, close the door and allow the heat of the oven to continue drying.

Blueberry-Orange Scones

Makes 6 – 8 scones

Be sure to have some extra blueberries on hand for your kitchen assistants to nibble while they work.

INGREDIENTS:

Scone batter:

- 3 cup self-rising flour (or all-purpose flour + 2 tablespoons baking powder)
- 1/2 cup sugar
- 1/2 cup butter
- 1 cup dried or fresh blueberries
- Grated peel of one orange
- 1 cup buttermilk
- 1/4 cup orange juice

Glaze:

- 1 cup powdered sugar
- 2–3 tablespoons orange juice

DIRECTIONS:

Preheat oven to 400 ° F.

Combine flour and sugar. Cut in butter until mixture is coarse and crumbly. Add blueberries and orange peel. Combine buttermilk and orange juice. Add just enough of the liquid mixture to make a soft dough. Turn out on a floured board and cut with a biscuit ring or large cookie cutter.

Place scones close together on a cookie sheet lined with baking parchment. Bake at 400 ° F. until lightly browned, about 10 minutes. Brush with glaze while still hot.

Chunky Apple Scones
Makes 10 – 12 small scones

INGREDIENTS:

- 2 cups whole wheat flour
- 2 teaspoons baking powder
- 1/2 cup brown sugar
- 1 teaspoon cinnamon
- 1/2 teaspoon nutmeg
- 1/2 cup butter
- 2 tart apples
- 1 large egg, beaten
- 1/2 teaspoon vanilla

DIRECTIONS:

Preheat oven to 375 ° F.

Grease and flour a baking pan.

Mix the flour, baking powder, cinnamon and nutmeg. Cut in the butter with a fork or pastry knife until the mixture is evenly crumbly. Peel, core and finely dice apples. Fold into the flour mixture. Then add the beaten egg.

Form the scones by lightly pressing them into egg-sized balls in your hands. Flatten them on the prepared baking sheet. Bake for 25 minutes or until the surface of the scones begins to brown.

Serve warm; plain or with butter and jam.

To reheat, split and toast in a toaster or return to a hot oven. Do not microwave.

Mandarin Orange Scones

Makes about 15 scones

INGREDIENTS:

Scones:

- 3 cups all-purpose flour
- 2 tablespoons baking powder
- 1/2 cup granulated sugar
- 1 stick of unsalted butter
- 1/2 to 3/4 cup buttermilk
- 1/4 cup mandarin oranges pureed in food processor
- Zest of one orange
- 1/4 cup mandarin orange segments, cut in half

Glaze:

- 1 cup powdered sugar
- 3 tablespoons orange juice

DIRECTIONS:

Preheat oven to 400 ° F.

Mix together flour and sugar. Use pastry cutter to cut in butter. Mixture should resemble coarse cornmeal.

Add zest, pureed mandarins and mandarin segments. Add enough of the buttermilk to make the mixture come together. If mixture is too dry add more buttermilk until it barely holds together.

Turn out on a floured board. Pat out to 1 inch thick. Cut with a small biscuit cutter or into triangles.

Bake for 15–20 minutes, or until nicely browned. Glaze when cool.

Glaze:

Mix together powdered sugar and orange juice. Dip scones in glaze. Let set until glaze is dry.

From Amy Lawrence at An Afternoon To Remember, *Newcastle, CA*

Applesauce Muffins

Makes 8 – 12 muffins

These muffins are very moist and slightly chewy and keep well in lunch boxes and picnic baskets.

INGREDIENTS:

- 1 cup applesauce
- 1/2 cup oil
- 2 eggs
- 3 tablespoons milk
- 2 cups flour
- 1 cup sugar
- 1/2 teaspoon baking powder
- 1 teaspoon cinnamon
- 1/2 teaspoon salt
- Cupcake baking liners

Muffin tins can be greased and floured if you do not use baking liners.

DIRECTIONS:

Preheat oven to 350 ° F.

Combine the wet ingredients and mix thoroughly. Combine the dry ingredients then add to the wet. Fold in gently. Do not over-mix. Spoon the batter into lined muffin tins. Bake about 15 – 20 minutes, until the top springs back to touch.

The Muffin Man Song

Oh do you know the muffin man,
The muffin man, the muffin man?
Oh do you know the muffin man,
That lives on Drury Lane?
Yes I know the muffin man,
The muffin man, the muffin man.
Yes I know the muffin man,
That lives on Drury Lane.

Pumpkin Spice Bread

Makes one loaf

*My first visit to a tearoom was to The Pear Tree in Pearland, Texas.
A bread recipe similar to this was served with a cream cheese filling as one
of the finger sandwiches. That day is one of my favorite memories of a gathering
with four generations of the women of my family. I'm pleased to say that
The Pear Tree is still in business today, serving tea and memories.*

INGREDIENTS:

- 1/2 cup softened butter
- 1 cup brown sugar
- 2 large eggs
- 1 cup canned pumpkin
- 1/2 cup buttermilk
- 1teaspoon vanilla
- 2 cups all-purpose flour
- 1 teaspoon baking powder
- 2 teaspoons baking soda
- 1/2 teaspoon salt
- 1 teaspoon ground cinnamon
- 1/2 teaspoon ground cloves
- 1/2 teaspoon ground mace
- 1/2 teaspoon ground ginger

DIRECTIONS:

Preheat oven to 350 ° F. Grease and flour a large loaf pan.

In a large bowl, cream together butter, sugar and one egg. When smooth, add second egg. Then add pumpkin, buttermilk and vanilla. Mix well. In a second bowl, stir together dry ingredients. Add to the pumpkin mixture and fold in just to moisten thoroughly. Do not over mix. Pour into the prepared pan.

Note: *Sandwiches are easier to make when the bred has had time to sit — not just out of the oven. And the sandwich fillings need to be very spreadable.*

Sandwich filling suggestions: Plain Cream Cheese, Carrot-Nut Sandwich Filling, page 60 and Triple Butter Sandwiches, page 58.

Sweet Popovers

Makes approximately 6 popovers

Popovers are fun to watch bake and delicious to eat.
This recipe is slightly sweet, intended for a fruit or dessert filling.
Eliminating the sugar would make it more compatible with a savory filling.

INGREDIENTS:

- 2 cups half-and-half, at room temperature
- 2 cups bread flour
- 1/4 cup white powdered sugar
- 3/4 teaspoon salt
- 1/2 teaspoon baking powder
- 3 large eggs, warmed to room temperature
- 2 tablespoon melted butter
- 1/2 teaspoon vanilla extract
- Light vegetable oil

DIRECTIONS:

In a large bowl, sift the flour, salt, and baking powder together. In a blender combine the eggs, milk, melted butter and vanilla. Process until eggs are completely blended. Add flour mixture to egg mixture in blender. Process briefly until ingredients are just combined. Some small lumps should remain. Allow the batter to rest for 30 minutes before pouring into the cups. Do not refrigerate the batter. It should be cooked immediately.

Preheat oven to 450 ° F. Heat an un-greased popover pan (muffin pan) at the same time.

When the batter is ready to bake and the oven is up to temperature, have the vegetable oil ready so that it can be brushed quickly in the baking cups. Coat the entire cup – bottom and sides. Fill the cups 3/4 full. Bake without opening the door for 15 minutes. Reduce heat to 375 ° F. Bake for another 25 minutes or until deep golden brown on the outside and airy on the inside.

Remove popovers from the oven, and cool on a rack. Pierce the sides with a sharp knife to let steam escape. Serve immediately with condiments or filling of choice. Popovers can be filled with any flavor mousse or sweet sandwich fillings such as Matcha Mousse, page 120 or Choco-Nut Sandwich Spread, page 65.

Corny Bread Muffins

Makes 6 – 8 muffins

INGREDIENTS:

Cornbread:

- 1 cup yellow cornmeal
- 1 cup all-purpose flour
- 1 tablespoon baking powder
- 1/2 teaspoon baking soda
- 3 tablespoons sugar
- 1/2 teaspoon salt
- 1 cup buttermilk
- 1 egg
- 1/3 cup melted butter
- Cupcake baking liners

Filling:

- 1 cup heavy cream
- 1 beaten egg
- 1 cup grated cheddar cheese
- 1 cup fresh or frozen corn

DIRECTIONS:

Preheat oven to 350 ° F.

Line each section of the muffin pan with the baking liners.

Mix the filling ingredients; set aside. In a large mixing bowl, combine the dry cornbread ingredients thoroughly. Make a well in the center of the dry mix and add the buttermilk, melted butter and egg. Mix until the egg is well blended with buttermilk then stir all the ingredients together.

Fill each muffin paper half-full with the cornbread mixture. Spoon a layer of the filling gently over the bottom layer of cornbread. Gently spoon the top layer of cornbread mixture over the filling. Bake 20 – 25 minutes, until golden brown.

Vegetable Sandwich Bread
Makes 1 loaf

INGREDIENTS:

- 2 eggs
- 2/3 cup oil
- 1 1/2 cups flour
- 3/4 teaspoon baking soda
- 1 teaspoon cinnamon
- 1/2 teaspoon salt
- 1 cup finely grated raw carrots
- 1 cup finely grated zucchini
- 1 cup chopped walnuts
- 1 cup finely grated apples

DIRECTIONS:

Preheat oven to 350 ° F.

Beat eggs and add oil. Sift together flour, soda, and salt. Add to egg mixture. Beat well. Add carrots, zucchini and nuts.

Grease a 9x5 inch loaf pan and pour in batter.

Bake one hour until the loaf is lightly browned and an inserted toothpick comes out clean. Let it cool completely before cutting slices for sandwiches.

Recommended sandwich fillings:

Carrot-Nut, page 60 and it's also great as a grilled cheese sandwich. Toast this bread lightly or grill with almost any kind of cheese under a hot broiler.

Cheese Crusts
Makes about 24 crackers

INGREDIENTS:

- 1 cup butter
- 1 cup sour cream
- 2 1/2 flour
- 1 teaspoon salt
- 1 teaspoon paprika
- 2 cup cheddar cheese, grated
- Baking parchment

DIRECTIONS:

Cream the butter and sour cream together. Add flour, salt and paprika. Knead it into a firm dough. During the final few minutes of kneading, add the cheese and mix evenly throughout the dough. Wrap or cover and refrigerate for one hour.

Preheat the oven to 350 º F.

Prepare a cookie sheet with parchment paper.

On a lightly floured board, roll the dough to about ¼ inch thick. Cut the dough into your favorite shapes. Bake for 15 minutes or until the edges begin to brown.

These are served like crackers. But they are delicious when still slightly warm.

Green Cheese

Green cheese, Yellow laces,
Up and down the market places.

An anonymous children's rhyme

Homemade Crackers
Makes approximately 24 crackers

INGREDIENTS:

- 1 1/2 cups whole wheat flour
- 1 1/2 cups all-purpose flour
- 1 teaspoon salt
- 1 cup warm water
- 1/3 cup olive oil
- 1/4 cup sesame seeds

DIRECTIONS:

In a large mixing bowl, whisk together the flours and salt. Add the water and olive oil. Knead by hand in the bowl. The dough should be just a bit tacky — not too dry, but not too sticky to work with. Add small portions of flour or water if needed to work the dough.

Cut the ball of dough into 6 sections. Rub each section with a bit of olive oil, set on a plate at room temperature and cover with a clean towel for one hour.

While the dough is resting, preheat your oven to 450°F.

Roll the dough on a floured surface, approximately ¼" thick, and then cut into your desired shapes. Sprinkle with sesame seeds (or other seed/herb topping of your choice). Bake for about 7 minutes until golden brown. Cool before eating.

Activity:

Children can use cookie cutters to cut favorite shapes for their crackers. Or, they can use toothpicks to draw their design on the dough and an adult can make the final cut with a paring knife.

Yeast Breads

Hot Cross Buns
Cranberry-Walnut Yeast Scones
Cinnamon Spiral Bread
Crumpets
Alphabet Bread Sticks

Hot Cross Buns

Makes 20 – 24 buns

INGREDIENTS:

Buns:

- 1 cup slightly warm milk
- 2 packages yeast
- 1/2 cup sugar
- 2 teaspoons salt
- 1/3 cup melted butter
- 1 teaspoon cinnamon
- 1/2 teaspoons nutmeg
- 4 c. crushed graham crackers
- 1 c. melted butter
- 4 eggs
- 5 cups flour
- 1 1/3 cups currants or raisins
- 1 egg white, beaten frothy

Glaze:

- 1 1/3 cups powdered sugar
- 1 1/2 teaspoons lemon zest
- 1/2 teaspoons lemon extract
- 1–2 tablespoons milk

DIRECTIONS:

Separate one of the eggs and save the egg white aside as a wash.

Pour warm milk in a mixing bowl and sprinkle yeast on the surface. Let sit to

dissolve for 5 minutes. Mix in sugar, salt, butter, cinnamon, nutmeg and eggs. Gradually add enough flour to make the dough elastic but still a bit sticky. Turn it out onto a floured surface and knead by hand until it is smooth. Knead in currants or raisins. Shape dough in a ball.

Line a baking sheet with parchment paper. Cut dough into pieces by cutting the ball into halves and then each piece into halves again. Shape each portion into a ball and place on the lined baking sheet, about 1/2 inch apart. Cover with a clean kitchen towel and let rise in a warm, draft-free place until doubled in size, about 1 1/2 hours.

To Bake:

Preheat oven to 350 ° F.

When buns have risen, take a sharp or serrated knife and slash with a cross. Brush them with the beaten egg white. Bake for 25 minutes or until golden. Cool slightly. Then glaze.

Glaze:

Whisk together glaze ingredients, and spoon over buns allowing the

glaze to fill the cross pattern.

Hot Cross Buns

Hot cross buns,
Hot cross buns,
One a penny,
Two a penny,
Hot Cross Buns

If you have no daughters,
Give them to your sons,
One a penny,
Two a penny,
Fresh, sweet buns.

Good Friday comes this month
The old woman runs
With one-a-penny,
Two-a-penny,
Hot Cross buns

Cranberry Walnut Yeast Scones

Makes 6 – 8 scones

*Most scones use a combination of eggs, baking powder and baking soda for leavening.
But working with yeast breads is like a bit of kitchen magic with children.
Most young children love to have their hands in the dough and delight in
watching the dough double in bulk. They take a bit longer and require
some planning — from which we all practice the skill of patience.*

*Yeast scones have a slightly different texture than quick bread versions.
The baked scone is less like a crumbly biscuit and more like a slice of bread.
It can be sliced and toasted without the tendency to fall apart.*

INGREDIENTS:

Scone Batter:

- 1/8 cup slightly warm water
- 2 envelopes active dry yeast
- 1 teaspoon sugar + ½ cup sugar
- 2 1/2 cups all-purpose flour
- 1 teaspoon baking soda
- 1 teaspoon salt
- 1 teaspoon cinnamon
- 1/2 teaspoon nutmeg
- 1/2 cup butter, softened
- 1 cup buttermilk
- 2 eggs
- 1 cup dried cranberries
- 1 cup walnuts, chopped
- Grated peel from one orange

Glaze:

- Juice of one orange
- 1 tablespoon melted butter
- 1 cup powdered sugar

DIRECTIONS:

Pour the warm water into a small bowl. Stir in the sugar and sprinkle yeast over the surface. Let proof 10 minutes. The mixture will start to froth when ready.

In a large bowl combine flour, baking soda, salt, cinnamon and nutmeg. Cut in butter until mixture resembles coarse crumbs. Beat in the eggs and add buttermilk. Gradually add in yeast mixture and buttermilk mixture to the dry ingredients, stirring just until the dough is barely moistened. Do not over-mix. Grate the orange peel. Stir in grated orange peel, cranberries and walnuts, cover and refrigerate at least 1 hour or at least doubled in bulk.

To Bake:

Preheat oven to 450 ° F.

Turn dough out onto a lightly floured surface and knead 3 – 4 times. Flatten to 1/2 inch thick circle. Score the surface like pie wedges or cut with cookie cutters. Place on un-greased baking sheet and let rise for 10 minutes. Bake until golden, about 15 – 20 minutes. Remove from the oven and cool for about 10 minutes. Prepare the glaze and drizzle it on the scones while they are still warm.

Scones are best when served warm.

Serve hot with butter or

Mock Devonshire Cream, page 129

Lemon Curd, page 129

or a favorite jam.

Cinnamon Spiral Bread

Makes 2 loaves

INGREDIENTS:

Bread Dough:

- 2 packages of dry yeast
- 2 cups of milk
- 1/4 cup sugar
- 2 teaspoons salt
- 1/2 cup melted butter
- 5 cups all purpose flour
- Additional flour for kneading
- 1 1/2 cups quick oatmeal, uncooked
- 1 egg, separated
- A splash of cold water

Filling:

- 1/2 cup sugar
- 2 tablespoons cinnamon

DIRECTIONS:

Separate the egg. Save the egg white for a wash and beat the yolk.

Soften yeast in lukewarm water and set aside. Scald the milk. Pour scalded milk over sugar, salt and butter. Cool to lukewarm. Add the beaten egg yolk. Stir in 1 cup of the flour. Stir in the softened yeast. Then add the oats. Gradually add enough additional flour to make an elastic dough.

Turn out on lightly floured board or canvas; knead until smooth, about 10 minutes. Divide dough into two balls. Roll one half to form a ½" thick rectangle. Sprinkle with half of filling made by combining sugar and cinnamon. Starting with short side, roll up as for jellyroll. Pinch the ends together. Repeat with other half of dough. Cover and let rise in warm place until double in size, about 1 hour.

Preheat oven to 425 ° F.

Beat the egg white with the splash of cold eater. Brush risen loaves with egg white wash.

Bake bread at 425°F for 15 minutes. Reduce oven temperature to 375°F.

Bake 25 – 30 minutes longer until the top is golden brown and tapping the surface produces a hollow sound.

Makes great sandwiches with:

Nutty-Fruity Filling, page 59

Carrot-Nut Filling, page 60

Triple Butter Sandwich, page 58.

Your Notes

Crumpets

Makes approximately 24 crumpets

INGREDIENTS:

- 2 packages dry yeast
- 1 teaspoon sugar
- 3 cups warm water
- Butter or margarine
- 2 tablespoons baking powder
- 4 cups all-purpose flour
- 2 teaspoons salt
- Crumpet Rings or small cans (both top and bottom cut out and washed thoroughly)
- Metal cookie cutters in simple shapes (optional)

DIRECTIONS:

Dissolve the yeast and sugar in the warm water. In a separate bowl, mix the flour, baking powder and salt. Add the dry mixture to the yeast water and whisk together.

Heat a heavy skillet or griddle to a medium-high heat. Grease the pan and the inside of the rings with butter or margarine. Place the rings in the hot skillet. Ladle the batter into the rings slowly, approximately ½" deep. Cook until the bubbles form and begin to break on the surface.

If you are using the metal cookie cutters to make different shapes, you should choose ones that don't have too many small details of the design. Grease the inside of the cookie cutters and put them into the greased pan. Pull the ring up with a fork or tongs. Remove the rings and turn the crumpet with a spatula to brown the other side.

Crumpets are most frequently split through the middle and toasted unless they are served piping hot, immediately after cooking. Serve with butter and jam or lemon curd.

Serve with Lemon Curd, page 129 or a favorite jam.

Alphabet Bread Sticks

Makes 12 – 24 letters

INGREDIENTS:

- 1 package dry yeast
- 2 cups slightly warm water
- 2 teaspoons salt
- 5 cups sifted all-purpose flour
- 1 tablespoon olive oil
- 2 tablespoons soft butter
- 1 egg, well beaten
- 1 tablespoon cold water

DIRECTIONS:

Soften the yeast in ¼ cup warm water. Let stand for 5 minutes. In a separate large mixing bowl put the 1¾ warm water. Add the salt and then gradually add 3 cups of the flour. Blend well. Stir in the yeast and mix well.

Add 1 cup more flour and the olive oil. Work until smooth, shiny and elastic; adding additional flour if necessary. Shape the dough into a ball and place it into a buttered bowl to rise. Cover the dough with butter to seal the exposed surface. Set aside in a draft-free location, cover with a clean dishtowel. It should take approximately 30 minutes to rise double in bulk.

Preheat oven to 425 °F.

Punch the dough down and knead again on a floured board or canvas until the dough is firm enough to be "worked". Pinch small portions out for each letter. Roll the dough into a thin coils. Shape the letters with the coils and place on prepared baking sheets. This can be greased or covered with baking parchment.

Mix the egg with the cold water until the mixture is frothy. Brush the letters with the egg mixture. Let rise, covered, in a warm place until doubled in bulk. Bake at 425° F for five minutes. Reduce oven temperature to 350° and bake for 10–15 minutes longer or until they are golden brown.

Cool before serving.

Cakes & Pies

Little Jack Horner's Pie
Blackbird Pie
Upside-Down Gingerbread Pear Cake
Lotsa Lemon Layer Cake
Blueberry Breakfast Cake
Fresh Berry Pie

Little Jack Horner's Pie

Serves 6 – 8

INGREDIENTS:

Pie Filling:

- 2 cups peeled & pitted red or purple plums **
- 2 cups peeled and finely diced baking apples
- 1 cup sugar
- 1/4 cup flour
- 1/4 teaspoon salt
- 1 teaspoon cinnamon
- 1 tablespoon lemon juice
- 1 unbaked 9-inch deep-dish pie crust (or your homemade crust)

** *The plum peeling can be bitter when cooked. It is usually better to peel the plums. One easy way is to soak the plums in a hot water bath for about 5 minutes and then peel with a sharp paring knife. There is no need to chop the plum meat. This is one of the adult jobs.*

Streusel Topping:

- 1/2 cup sugar
- 1/2 cup flour
- ½ cup quick, uncooked oats
- 1/2 teaspoon cinnamon
- 1/4 teaspoon nutmeg
- 4 tablespoons cold butter

DIRECTIONS:

Preheat oven to 375 ° F.

Combine the plums, diced apples, sugar, flour, salt, cinnamon and lemon juice. Stir together. Pour into the unbaked pastry shell.

Prepare the topping by combining sugar, flour, oats, cinnamon and nutmeg. Blend together. Then cut in the cold butter until it is in coarse clumps.

Sprinkle the topping over the fruit filling.

Bake for one hour or until the fruit filling begins to bubble through the topping and the crust rim is golden brown. If the crust begins to brown too quickly, you can wrap the rim with strips of aluminum foil.

Cool before serving.

Little Jack Horner

Little Jack Horner sat in the corner
Eating his Christmas pie,
He put in his thumb and pulled out a plum
And said "What a good boy am I!"

Black Bird Pie

Serves 6 – 8

This simple recipe uses simple ingredients in a fun way. If you don't want to make your own filling, you can use a commercial pie filling – your favorite flavor!

INGREDIENTS:

- 3/4 c. sugar
- 1/3 c. flour
- 1/2 t. salt
- 2 c. milk
- 2 eggs
- 1 tablespoon butter
- 1/2 c. semi sweet chocolate chips
- 1 teaspoon vanilla
- 1 baked and cooled pie shell or a cookie crumb crust
- 1 recipe of Homemade Whipped Cream, page 128
- 1 recipe of Gingerbread People, page 38

DIRECTIONS:

Make the recipe of Gingerbread People, but cut in the shapes of birds and bake according to the directions. These can be made ahead of time.

Make or purchase the pie shell.

FILLING:

In a saucepan whisk together sugar, flour and salt. Add 1 cup of milk and mix until smooth. Bring to boil over medium heat, stirring briskly. Continue until smooth and thick — about 2 minutes. Remove from heat. With fork, beat eggs with remaining milk; gradually stir into hot mixture, then put back over heat. Bring to a boil, stirring constantly and boil until mixture thickens a bit, about 1 minute. Remove from heat. Stir in butter, chocolate chips and vanilla. Stir until chocolate is melted. Pour into pie shell. Chill for at least 2 hours before cutting.

Make the recipe of Homemade Whipped Cream, or use a commercial whipped topping.

Immediately before serving, decorate the top of the pie with the gingerbread birds. The Gingerbread Birds begin to soften in the pie filling so they cannot remain as decorations for long. As you serve the pie and enjoy the nursery rhyme, you might want to remove any un-served birds to save for later.

Sing A Song Of Sixpence

Sing a song of sixpence,
A pocket full of rye;
Four and twenty blackbirds
Baked in a pie.
When the pie was opened,
They all began to sing.
Now, wasn't that a dainty dish
To set before the King?

The King was in his counting house,
Counting out his money;
The Queen was in the parlor
Eating bread and honey.
The maid was in the garden,
Hanging out the clothes.
Along there came a big black bird
And snipped off her nose!

Upside-Down Gingerbread Pear Cake

Serves 12

INGREDIENTS:

The Pears:

- 4–5 fresh pears, peeled, cored and sliced into thin strips
- 2 tablespoons flour for dusting the pears
- 1 cup apple juice

The Cake:

- 2 cups all-purpose flour
- 1/2 cup brown sugar
- 1/2 cup quick oats
- 1 tablespoon ground ginger
- 2 tablespoons crystallized ginger, chopped
- 1 teaspoon baking soda
- 1/2 cup corn syrup
- 1/2 cup molasses
- 1/2 cup milk
- 1/2 cup butter, softened

DIRECTIONS:

Pre-heat oven to 350° F.

Grease a 9 x 13" baking pan.

Prepare the pear slices, save in a small mixing bowl and toss with the 2 tablespoons of flour to coat the apples. Add apple juice and set aside.

Combine the flour, sugar, oats, ground ginger and crystallized ginger together in a large mixing bowl. Make a well in the center. Melt the butter in a saucepan. Add the syrup and molasses. Heat only until warm. Do not boil. Pour the butter mixture into the well of the dry ingredients. Drop the baking soda on top and then sprinkle the vinegar over the soda. It's great fun to watch it fizz.

Add the milk to the mixture in the well and mix thoroughly. This should be a loose batter. Spread the pear mixture evenly in the bottom of the prepared baking pan. Pour the batter over the pears and bake for 1 hour.

When the top becomes dark brown and a bit shiny, test for doneness by touching the center. It should spring back when completely done.

This is best served warm but is also very tasty cold. To serve, cut the cake into squares. Lift out the squares and turn them over on the plate so that the pears are on the top. Serve plain or with Homemade Whipped Cream, page 128 or Mock Devonshire Cream, page 129.

Your Notes

Lotsa Lemon Layer Cake

Serves 8 – 10

Special occasion desserts with many ingredients and several steps are often the best times to share the kitchen and a sense of accomplishment with your child.

INGREDIENTS:

Lemon Curd Filling:

- 3 egg yolks
- 1/3 cup sugar
- 6 tablespoons of butter
- Zest of one lemon
- 1/2 cup lemon juice (2–3 lemons)

Cake:

- 1/2 cup butter
- 1/2 cup shortening
- 1 1/2 cup sugar
- 3 eggs, beaten
- 1 cup buttermilk
- 2 1/4 cup cake flour
- 1/2 teaspoon salt
- 1 teaspoon baking soda
- 1/4 cup lemon juice (1–2 lemons)

Frosting:

- 1 box powdered sugar
- 1 stick of butter, softened
- 1/4 cup half and half
- Zest from 1 lemon
- 1 teaspoon lemon extract

DIRECTIONS:

Lemon Curd Filling:

In a saucepan, whisk egg yolks together with sugar and zest. Add lemon juice and butter. Whisk gently over medium heat until the mixture is thick. Cool in a separate small bowl.

Cake:

Preheat oven to 350 ° F. Grease and flour two 8-inch round cake pans. Cream together butter, shortening and sugar. Add in sugar and then beat in eggs one at a time. The mixture will become light and fluffy.

Into a separate bowl sift together flour, salt and soda. Spoon half the flour mixture gently onto the batter and fold it in gradually. Fold in buttermilk and lemon juice. Then fold in the remaining flour mixture. Pour the batter into the pans. Tap gently on the counter top to release air bubbles.

Bake for 20 minutes or until the tops begin to brown and the center springs back to touch. Remove from baking pans. Cool on wire racks.

Frosting:

Beat ingredients together with an electric mixer just before assembling the cake.

Assemble the cake:

When cool, trim the rounded top to flatten the cake for stacking. Put a bit of the lemon curd on the surface of the plate to stabilize the cake. Center the first layer of cake on the plate. Spread the top of the first layer with a thin coating of the frosting. Add a generous layer of lemon curd as the filling. Position the top layer. Frost the outside of the cake.

Blueberry Breakfast Cake
Serves 8 – 12

INGREDIENTS:

- 2 cups brown sugar
- 2 cups flour
- 1/2 cup butter
- 1 teaspoon baking soda
- 1/2 teaspoon salt
- 1 egg, beaten
- 1 cup buttermilk
- 1 teaspoon vanilla extract
- 1/2 teaspoon ground nutmeg
- 2 teaspoons cinnamon
- 1 cup chopped walnuts
- 1 cup blueberries; fresh, frozen or dehydrated**
- 1 recipe Fresh Blueberry Sauce, page 130 (optional)

** **Note:** *Canned blueberries can be used if well drained.*

DIRECTIONS:

Preheat oven to 350 º F. Grease and flour a 9 x 13" baking pan.

In a mixing bowl, sift together the flour, baking soda, salt, nutmeg and cinnamon. Combine brown sugar and flour mixture. Mix in butter with hands or with a pastry knife until the mixture is crumbly. Add the chopped nuts. Remove 1/2 cup of this mixture and set aside as a topping.

Add beaten egg, buttermilk and vanilla to the remaining mixture in the bowl. Stir well. Gently fold in the blueberries and pour mixture into the prepared baking pan. Sprinkle topping over the surface.

Bake for 30 minutes or until the center of the cake springs back to touch.

Serve plain or with Fresh Blueberry Sauce. Is best eaten slightly warm but keeps well for 2–3 days if covered.

Fresh Berry Pie

Makes 8 – 10 servings

INGREDIENTS:

Pie Filling:

- 1 homemade or purchased 9-inch crumb pie crust, see below
- 6 cups fresh mixed berries, divided (sauce & filling)
- 1/4 cup sugar
- 2 tablespoons water
- 2 tablespoons cornstarch
- 1/4 cup cold water
- 1 tablespoon butter
- 1 tablespoon lemon juice
- Homemade Whipped Cream, page 128 or purchased whipped topping

Cookie Crust:

- 2 cups fine vanilla wafer crumbs
- 1/2 cup melted butter
- 1/3 cup sugar

DIRECTIONS:

Cookie Crust:

Preheat oven to 400 ° F.

Combine vanilla wafer crumbs, sugar and melted butter. Press over bottom and up sides of 9-inch pie plate. Bake at 400 degrees F for 10 minutes. Cool completely.

Filling:

Combine 2 cups berries, sugar and 2 tablespoons water in large saucepan; bring to a full boil. Dissolve cornstarch in 1/4 cup cold water; add to berry mixture. Return to the boil, stirring constantly. Reduce heat to low and cook, stirring, for 2 minutes. Remove from heat. Stir in butter, lemon juice and remaining 4 cups of berries. Spoon into crumb crust. Let stand 3 hours until set. Serve with Whipped Cream or commercial whipped topping. It is best to add the topping just before serving.

Tip: *Save some whole berries to decorate the top.*

Puddings

Plain Pudding
Lemon Pudding
Traditional English Trifle
Berry Trifle Cups
Matcha Mint Mousse
Baked Spiced Custard
Old Fashioned Hasty Pudding
Figgy Pudding With Custard Sauce

Plain Pudding

Serves 4

*Pudding is one of the ultimate comfort foods and
can be very soothing to someone with a sore throat.*

INGREDIENTS:

- 2 cups milk
- 1/2 cup sugar
- 3 tablespoons cornstarch
- 1/4 teaspoon salt
- 1 teaspoon vanilla extract
- 1 tablespoon butter

DIRECTIONS:

Heat milk in a saucepan over medium heat until bubbles form at edges. In a bowl, mix sugar, cornstarch and salt. Pour into hot milk, a spoon-full at a time. Stir each addition to dissolve.

Continue to cook and stir until mixture thickens enough to coat the back of a teaspoon, about 8–10 minutes. Do not boil. Remove from heat, stir in vanilla and butter. Pour into serving dishes.

Chill before serving.

Variations:

Pudding cups can be topped with chopped fresh fruit or used to make A Traditional English Trifle, page 118.

Pudding can become a beautiful parfait. Layer pudding and fresh fruit in a glass or make layers of different flavored pudding. See Lemon Pudding, page 117.

Plain Pudding can quickly become chocolate by melting chocolate chips in before cooling.

Lemon Pudding

Serves 4 – 6

Sometimes Lemon Curd is a bit too heavy.
This Lemon Pudding is a bit lighter on the butter
but just as tangy with fresh lemon flavor.

INGREDIENTS:

- 3/4 cup sugar
- 1/4 cup cornstarch
- 2 1/2 cups milk
- 3 egg yolks, beaten
- 2 tablespoons softened butter
- 2 tablespoons lemon zest
- 1/4 teaspoon salt
- 1/2 cup fresh lemon juice

DIRECTIONS:

Whisk the sugar and the cornstarch together in a medium saucepan. Add the milk and whisk until smooth.

Add the egg yolks, zest, and salt. Mix well and cook over medium heat. Stir frequently at first and constantly towards the end, until thick enough to coat the back of a spoon.

Remove the pan from the heat and stir in the lemon juice and butter. If there are lumps, pour through a strainer into the individual serving dishes.

Refrigerate to chill before serving.

Serve plain or with fresh fruit.

Tip: *You can create an elegant parfait by layering fresh fruit and pudding.*
Adding additional layers of cubed cake is the basis for a Trifle. See Traditional Trifle,
page 118.

Traditional English Trifle

Serves 6 – 8

This no-bake recipe is easy and fun. Even young children can take the lead in creating this elegant dessert.

It can be made in one large glass bowl or in small individual glasses.
The glass serving dish is important to show the colorful layers.

INGREDIENTS:

- 4 cups of cubed white cake or sponge cake (1" cubes)
- 4 cups fresh strawberries
- 1/4 cup white sugar
- 1 pint fresh blueberries
- 2 bananas
- 1/4 cup orange juice
- 1 recipe of Plain Pudding, page 116
- 1 cup heavy whipping cream
- 1/4 cup blanched slivered almonds
- 1 small bottle maraschino cherries

DIRECTIONS:

Slice strawberries and sprinkle them with sugar. Cut the bananas into slices and toss with orange juice. Use half of the cake cubes to line the bottom of a large glass bowl. Layer half of the strawberries followed by half of the blueberries, and then half of the bananas. Spread half of the pudding over the fruit. Repeat layers in the same order.

In a separate bowl, whip the cream to stiff peaks and spread over top of trifle. Decorate the top with maraschino cherries and slivered almonds.

Cover and refrigerate until it is served.

Berry Trifle Parfait

Serves 6 – 8

During the summer blackberry season you may have buckets of the deep blue treats on hand. This quick dessert can be very simple or extremely elegant.

One Fourth of July specialty can be created by creating layers of dark blackberries with bright red strawberries.

INGREDIENTS:

- 1 recipe of Plain Pudding, page 116
- 4 cups of cubed white cake or sponge cake (*1" cubes*)
- 1/4 cup white sugar
- 4 cups fresh blackberries or strawberries – or a combination
- 1 cup heavy whipping cream
- 1 small bottle maraschino cherries (*cherries & juice*)

DIRECTIONS:

Prepare the pudding recipe and chill.

Prepare the berries and sprinkle with sugar. Cube the cake and sprinkle with some of the maraschino juice.

Select some interesting glasses in which you will create the parfait-style dessert.

Begin the layers with a few small cubes of cake in the bottom. Add fruit. Then pudding. Repeat until the glass is beautifully full.

Top with whipped cream just before serving.

Decorate the top with a maraschino cherry.

Note: *A parfait is like a trifle, but is usually served in individual glasses.*

Matcha Mint Mousse

Serves 4

Mousse is a soft, fluffy pudding.

INGREDIENTS:

- 1 teaspoon unflavored gelatin powder
- 4 tablespoons cool water
- 2 eggs, well beaten
- 1/2 cup sugar
- 1 cup milk
- 1 cup heavy cream, whipped to soft peaks
- 2 tablespoons matcha green tea powder
- 3 tablespoons warm water
- 1/4 teaspoon mint extract
- Fresh mint sprigs

DIRECTIONS:

Dissolve gelatin powder in the cold water and set aside. Whip the eggs until frothy and add sugar. Heat milk in a pan until lukewarm and add the beaten eggs. Whisk over low heat for one minute to cook the eggs. Then add the dissolved gelatin and whisk well. Remove from heat.

Dissolve the matcha tea powder in the warm water. Whisk the matcha into the egg and milk mixture. Allow mixture to cool. Fold it gradually into the whipped cream. Pour the mixture into cups or glasses and chill for 4 hours or overnight.

This is delicious served as a pudding or it can also be a filling for Sweet Popovers, page 87.

Matcha Note: *You can purchase Matcha from Asian grocery stores or specialty teashops. There are currently many online tea businesses that sell Matcha and other specialty teas. It is a bit expensive but offers many health benefits. It is extremely high in antioxident value and medical research is proving its value for many health issues. The taste is unusual and new to many of us. Recipes like this one might help our families develop the appreciation for matcha as we substitute it for less healthy ingredients.*

Baked Spiced Custard

Serves 4 – 6

INGREDIENTS:

Custard:

- 4 eggs
- 1/2 cup sugar
- 2 cups whole milk
- 1 tablespoon melted butter
- 1 teaspoon salt
- 1 teaspoon vanilla
- ½ teaspoon cinnamon
- ½ teaspoon nutmeg
- 2 tablespoons all-purpose flour

Streusel topping:

- 2 tablespoons all-purpose flour
- 2 tablespoons butter
- 4 tablespoons sugar
- ¼ cup quick oats (uncooked)

DIRECTIONS:

Preheat oven to 300 ° F.

Prepare custard:

Beat the eggs thoroughly. Beat in the other ingredients and whisk until smooth. Prepare the streusel topping by incorporating the flour, sugar and butter together with a fork until the mixture is crumbly. Then add the oats and mix.

Pour custard into an un-greased 9" square baking pan. A glass or ceramic pan seems to work best. Set the baking pan into a slightly larger pan. Fill the larger pan with water until it comes about half-way up the side of the custard pan. Sprinkle the topping on the surface of the liquid custard. Bake for 45 minutes.

Cut a small square for each person. Can be served with a Homemade Whipped Cream, page 128 or Mock Devonshire Cream, page 129.

Can be served warm or cold.

Old-Fashioned Hasty Pudding

Makes 4 – 6 servings

This recipe is titled with a bit of humor because it is not the least bit 'hasty'. But it does take us back in American history and is a fun dish to serve for afternoon tea.

INGREDIENTS:

- 4 cups milk
- 4 tablespoons cornmeal
- 1/2 cup brown sugar
- 1/2 cup waffle syrup
- 1 tablespoon butter
- 2 eggs, beaten
- 1 1/2 teaspoons cinnamon
- 1 teaspoon ginger
- 1/4 teaspoon nutmeg
- 1/4 teaspoon ground cloves
- 1/2 teaspoon salt
- 1/2 teaspoon baking soda

DIRECTIONS:

Preheat oven to 325 ° F.

In a heavy saucepan scald milk and cream. Gradually sprinkle with yellow cornmeal and bring to a boil, stirring constantly. When boiling, stir in sugar, maple syrup, butter and the 6 dry ingredients. Reduce heat. Simmer for 5 minutes. Let the mixture cool for 10 minutes.

Whisk the beaten eggs into the cooled milk mixture. Pour the batter into a buttered baking dish. Place the baking dish in a larger baking pan. Add water to the outer pan so that the filled casserole is surrounded by the water bath and keep it more than half full. Bake for 2 hours.

Can be scooped out of the baking dish or cut into squares.

Serve warm, plain or with your favorite toppings.

Yankee Doodle

Father and I went down to camp,
Along with Captain Goodin',
And there we saw the men and boys
As thick as hasty puddin'.

CHORUS:
Yankee Doodle keep it up,
Yankee Doodle dandy,
Mind the music and the step,
And with the girls be handy.

Figgy Pudding with Custard Sauce

Serves 10 – 12

Figgy Pudding is baked in the oven in a pan of water so that the steam keeps it moist. This is a traditional Christmas recipe in Great Britain, as in the carol.

INGREDIENTS:

For the pudding batter:

- 1/2 cup butter
- 1/2 cup shortening
- 1 cup sugar
- 3 large egg yolks
- 1 cup scalded milk
- 2 tablespoons vanilla
- 1 cup chopped walnuts
- 1/2 teaspoon cinnamon
- 1/4 teaspoon ground cloves
- 1/4 teaspoon ground ginger
- 1 1/2 cups dried breadcrumbs
- 2 teaspoons baking powder
- 1 apple, peeled and cored and finely chopped
- 1 pound dried figs, ground or finely chopped
- Grated peel of 1 lemon and 1 orange
- 3 large egg whites, stiffly beaten

For the custard sauce:

- 2 cups milk
- 1 large egg, beaten
- 3/4 cups sugar
- 1 teaspoon vanilla
- 1 tablespoon all-purpose flour
- 1 tablespoon butter

DIRECTIONS:

Prepare the pudding:

Preheat oven to 325 ° F. Generously grease an oven-proof 2-quart casserole dish or mold and set aside. Cream together butter and shortening. Gradually add the remaining ingredients except egg whites, mixing well after each addition. Fold stiffly beaten egg whites into mixture.

124

Pour into the baking dish and cover tightly with foil. Place into large shallow pan on middle rack in oven. Fill the shallow pan half-full with boiling water and slowly steam pudding in oven at 325 ° for 4 hours, replacing water as needed.

Prepare the custard sauce:

In saucepan, scald milk and allow to cool slightly. Mix together remaining ingredients, except butter. Add to milk. Cook over low heat until thickened. Remove from heat and stir in butter. Mix well.

We Wish You A Merry Christmas
16th Century English Christmas Carol

We wish you a Merry Christmas
We wish you a Merry Christmas
We wish you a Merry Christmas
and a Happy New Year.

REFRAIN
Good tidings we bring to you and your kin
We wish you a Merry Christmas and a Happy New Year.

Now bring us some figgy pudding
Now bring us some figgy pudding
Now bring us some figgy pudding
and bring some out here.
REFRAIN
For we all like figgy pudding
For we all like figgy pudding
For we all like figgy pudding
so bring some out here.

Sauces & Creams

Homemade Whipped Cream
Lemon Curd
Mock Devonshire Cream
Fresh Blueberry Sauce
Lemon Sauce
Simple Chocolate Cocoa Sauce
Butterscotch Sauce

Homemade Whipped Cream

Makes approximately 8 servings

Homemade whipped cream is quick and easy.

INGREDIENTS:

- 1 pint heavy whipping cream
- 1/2 teaspoon vanilla extract
- 1/4 cup powdered sugar

DIRECTIONS:

Chill the bowl and whipping cream. Whip the cream with an electric mixer. As it begins to thicken, gradually add powdered sugar.

Continue to mix for about 4 minutes. Add vanilla. The cream should be thick enough to form peaks that hold their shape when you pull the beaters out of the bowl.

A whisk can be used to whip the cream but it takes longer.

The whipped cream can be served immediately or kept in the refrigerator until needed. Cover to keep from absorbing other odors and flavors.

It can be stored, covered, for 2–3 days. But you may want to whisk it a bit just before serving.

Variations:

Substitute a few drops of a different flavoring syrup or extract.

Mix in a tablespoon of jam or jelly while whipping the cream.

Mix in 2 tablespoons dry hot chocolate mix powder.

Fold in chopped nuts or sprinkles just before serving.

Lemon Curd

Makes 1 1/2 cups; Serves 6 – 8

INGREDIENTS:

- 3/4 cup fresh lemon juice
- 1 tablespoon grated lemon zest
- 3/4 cup sugar
- 3 eggs
- 1/2 cup butter, cut into chunks

DIRECTIONS:

In a saucepan, combine lemon juice, lemon zest, sugar, eggs, and butter. Cook over low heat until thick, about 10 minutes. Cool before serving. Lemon curd can be kept covered and refrigerated for up to a week.

Mock Devonshire Cream

Makes approximately 6 – 8 servings

This is an imitation of a traditional topping that originated in Devon County, England.

INGREDIENTS:

- 1/4 cup cream cheese, room temperature
- 2 tablespoons brown sugar
- 1/8 teaspoon salt
- 3/4 cup whipping cream

DIRECTIONS:

In a large bowl, combine cream cheese, sugar, and salt. Mix well. Gradually add the whipping cream. This is most easily done with an electric mixer but it can be done by hand. Store covered in the refrigerator until ready to serve.

This is a traditional topping on warm scones. But there are many other uses.

It is delicious as a dip for fresh strawberries.

Fresh Blueberry Sauce

Makes approximately 6 – 8 servings

INGREDIENTS:

- 2 cups fresh blueberries
- 1/3 cup sugar
- 1 tablespoon fresh lemon juice
- 1/4 teaspoon salt
- 1/2 teaspoon vanilla extract

DIRECTIONS:

Wash and crush blueberries. Add sugar, lemon juice and salt. Mix well. In a small saucepan, bring blueberry mixture to a gentle simmer for 1 minute. Remove from heat. Add vanilla. Chill.

Serve over puddings, cake, or ice cream.

This makes a good topping for Blueberry Breakfast Cake, page 112.

Blueberries
By Robert Frost

Blueberries as big as the end of your thumb,
Real sky-blue, and heavy, and ready to drum
In the cavernous pail of the first one to come
And all ripe together, not some of them green
And some of them ripe! You ought to have seen!

Lemon Sauce

Makes approximately 8 servings

This Lemon Sauce recipe is another substitute for Lemon Curd. One difference between them is the amount of butter and number of eggs. Lemon sauce is thickened with cornstarch and is both lighter and less expensive.

INGREDIENTS:

- 1/4 cup cornstarch
- 1 cup sugar
- 1 cup water
- 2 eggs, well beaten
- 1/4 cup lemon juice
- Finely grated lemon peel of one lemon
- 1 tablespoon butter

DIRECTIONS:

Stir the cornstarch and sugar together in a saucepan. Add water and eggs. Mix well and then cook over medium heat, stirring frequently. Bring it to a boil (about 10 minutes).

Remove from heat and whisk it until it is smooth and thick and a bit cooler. Add lemon juice, lemon peel and butter. Whisk just until the butter is thoroughly melted.

Lemon sauce can be served warm with scones or spooned as a topping on crepes. In many recipes it can be a substitute for lemon curd.

Simple Cocoa Chocolate Sauce

Makes approximately 6 – 8 servings

INGREDIENTS:

- 2/3 cup unsweetened cocoa
- 1 cup sugar
- 1/4 cup water
- 1/2 cup white corn syrup
- 3/4 cup milk
- 1 teaspoon vanilla extract

DIRECTIONS:

Mix the dry cocoa and sugar together in a saucepan. Gradually add the water, corn syrup and milk. Bring to a simmer, stirring until the mixture is smooth. Let it simmer for 2–3 minutes, stirring occasionally.

Remove from heat and add the vanilla.

Butterscotch Sauce

Makes approximately 6 – 8 servings

INGREDIENTS:

- 3/4 cup light brown sugar, packed
- 1/2 cup light corn syrup
- 2 tablespoons butter
- 1/2 cup heavy whipping cream
- 1 teaspoon vanilla

DIRECTIONS:

Combine sugar, corn syrup and butter in a small saucepan. Bring it to a gentle simmer over low-to-medium heat, stirring constantly. Simmer gently for 2–3 minutes. Remove from heat. Whisk in cream and vanilla immediately.

Cool before serving. If you have any leftovers, store in the refrigerator for up to 2 weeks for up to two weeks.

You might want to serve this sauce on the Stuffed Baked Apples, page 51 and on Upside-down gingerbread Pear Cake, page 108.

Your Notes

High Tea

There are two very different styles of meal served and called High Tea. One meaning is intended to be very elaborate; a special occasion. The other meaning comes from Great Britain where High Tea refers to an evening meal when the family gathers at the end of the day. In contrast to the petit sandwiches and decorated cakes, the food served is warm and comfortable. The final recipes in Emma Lea's Family Cookbook are the soups and main courses that might be served for a family's evening meal . . . with a nice pot of tea!

I celebrate the idea that High Tea is Family Tea.
What better reason to celebrate?

Soups

"Here's Looking-At-You" Soup
Won Ton Soup
Make It My Way Soup
Stone Soup
Oats, Peas, Beans & Barley Soup

"Here's-Looking-At-You" Soup

Serves 4

INGREDIENTS:

- 1 tablespoon vegetable oil
- 1 small white onion, finely diced
- 1 clove of garlic, crushed and diced
- 2 cups chicken or vegetable stock – canned or homemade
- 4 medium-sized potatoes, peeled and cut into small cubes
- 1 cup half-and half (can also be regular milk)
- Salt to taste

DECORATIONS

These are a few suggestions. You can use your imagination to create something fun for your family. The following decorations are a few suggestions that make hair, eyes, lips, teeth, ears and a nose.

- Parsley, chopped
- Sliced black olives
- Stuffed green olives
- Grated cheddar cheese
- Slices of red & yellow pepper
- Cooked bacon, broken into pieces
- Chow mien noodles
- Cut shapes from lightly toasted bread

DIRECTIONS:

Heat oil in a medium-sized saucepan. Add onion and garlic and cook until softened. Add stock and potatoes. Cook uncovered until potatoes are soft. Add enough of the milk to cool the mixture. Pour it into the blender canister and whirl it until potatoes are crushed. This may need to be done in two separate batches. Add milk slowly until it is your desired consistency. Return the soup to the saucepan. Add salt if needed. Re-heat under very low heat just before serving. Serve soup in a low, wide bowl.

ACTIVITY:

Serve each guest a plain bowl of soup and demonstrate how to make a face with the decoration choices. Guests create their own soup funny face. Make sure the soup is not too hot when served so that young children aren't burned.

Won Ton Soup

Makes 4 – 6 servings

INGREDIENTS:

- 1 package won ton wrappers
- 1 pound ground turkey
- 1/4 cup finely ground bread crumbs
- 1 egg
- 1 teaspoon salt
- 2 green onions
- 6 cups clear broth (*chicken, vegetable stock or miso*)
- 1/4 cup slivers of carrot
- 1/2 cup thinly sliced celery

DIRECTIONS:

Won Tons:

Separate the egg yolk from the egg white. Beat the egg white until frothy and set aside. Mix the turkey with breadcrumbs, egg yolk and salt. In the center of each square won ton wrapper, place a small ball of the turkey mixture. Brush the beaten egg white along the inside edges of the won ton. Fold the wrapper closed, matching the moistened edges to form a triangular shaped pouch. Press together firmly. Bring the two points of the triangle together and fasten with a bit of the egg white mixture. Chill the won tons for one hour before cooking in the soup. You can also freeze them for use at a later date.

Soup:

Heat the broth with the onion, carrot and celery to a simmer. Cook until the vegetables are done to your taste. Bring it to a rolling boil. Add wontons by lowering them in with a long-handled spoon. Cook for about 4–5 minutes until the won tons are done. Serve immediately.

Options:

Add some other favorite chopped vegetables: broccoli, red bell peppers, spinach, bok choy, cabbage or bean sprouts.

Try your own filling ideas. Other meats, tofu and other vegetarian fillings all work well.

Make it My Way Soup

Makes 4 – 6 servings

This is a fun way to introduce your family to new foods.
It's easy to take a small trial portion of a new vegetable.
The preparation can begin at the market or in your own garden.

INGREDIENTS:

- 4 – 6 cups clear broth (beef, chicken, vegetable or miso)

Choose from the list of re-cooked, ready-to-serve ingredients. You can use any of your favorite soup ingredients. These are a few suggestions. Make sure they are ready-to-eat. And they should be warm or room temperature

- Meatballs from ground turkey
- Chopped cooked chicken
- Cubed tofu
- Won tons, recipe for homemade won tons on page 137
- Noodles or macaroni
- Chopped green onion tops
- Broccoli florettes
- Slivers or coins of carrot
- Chopped celery
- Green beans
- Green peas
- Slices of bok choy
- Fresh spinach leaves (can be added raw)
- Thinly sliced cabbage leaves
- Cubed fresh tomatoes or stewed tomatoes
- Cubed potato or small new potatoes
- Chopped parsley
- Kidney beans
- Grated parmesan cheese
- Crackers

DIRECTIONS:

Prepare all soup ingredients so that they are ready to serve. One of the easiest ways is to steam the vegetables or to blanche them in the soup broth.

Serve the soup by having the different ingredients available in separate small serving bowls. Each diner is served a bowl of clear broth. Then, each guest chooses the ingredients for their personal bowl.

Your Notes

Stone Soup

The story of Stone Soup is well known as a picture book. But you can create the same experience for young children with your own magic stone and interesting array of

ingredients.

INGREDIENTS:

- A magic stone
- A large soup pot
- Water
- Vegetables
- Optional soup bone or other meat products
- The Stone Soup picture book or a willing storyteller

DIRECTIONS:

There are many versions of this classic story. And you can easily find a picture book version at your local library or bookstore. I've composed a short version of the story here.

Begin by reading the story together. Follow with the suggestion to make your own stone soup. Be sure to wash and pre-boil your magic stone. Sometimes I've even tied a string around the stone so that we could lift it out to see it while it's cooking. That always produced lots of jokes and giggles. Then have your child help make the choices for what goes in next.

I encourage you to explain that the rock isn't really magic. It just makes the story fun and teaches us lessons about generosity and teamwork.

And while the soup is cooking, you can also make some Homemade Crackers, page 91 or Cheese Crusts, page 90, to serve together.

Note: *Adding meat to the soup requires a longer cooking time. If you want to use meat, you might be able to have the stock and meat cooked in advance if time is critical.*

The Story of Stone Soup

Once upon a time there was a land which had suffered from many years of war and the destruction of their land. Money and food were scarce. The people were careful and forced to live on very little. One day a wandering soldier came into the village looking for a place to stay.

"There's nothing to eat in our town," he was told. "Better find somewhere else to settle."

"Oh, I have everything I need," he said. "In fact, I can see how you are suffering and thought of making some soup for all of you." He pulled a kettle from his wagon, filled it with water, and built a fire under it. Then, with great ceremony, he drew an ordinary-looking stone from a silk bag and dropped it into the water.

News of the stranger traveled quickly through the village and many came to watch him prepare his mysterious soup. The soldier sniffed the broth and smacked his lips.

"Ahh," the soldier said to himself rather loudly, "I do like a tasty stone soup. Of course, stone soup with a beef bone — well, that's much better."

The butcher was standing at the edge of the town square and all eyes turned to him. "Well, I suppose I have a bone I could add to the pot."

The soldier added the meat bone with great ceremony and the townspeople cheered. Then he added, "You know, I once had stone soup with cabbage and a bit of salt beef as well, and it was fit for a king."

The farmer's wife happened to have an extra cabbage in her cart on the way to the market. "Well, since you're going to share with everyone, I can add this."

The soldier cut the cabbage with his knife and soon the other neighbors brought out potatoes, onions and carrots to add to the kettle.

The soup was delicious and the mayor of the town tried to buy the magical stone from the soldier. He refused to sell and traveled on the next day. The moral is that by working together, with everyone contributing what they can, a greater good is achieved.

Oats, Peas, Beans & Barley Soup
Makes 6 – 8 servings

INGREDIENTS:

- 1 meaty beef soup bone
- 1 bay leaf
- 6 beef bouillon cubes (or 6 cups beef stock)
- 1/2 cup barley
- 1/4 cup oatmeal
- 2 cups canned tomatoes
- 1/2 pound stewing beef, cubed
- 1 large onion, chopped
- 1/2 teaspoon thyme
- 1 teaspoon paprika
- 1 cup sliced carrot, 1/2" thick
- 2 potatoes, peeled and diced
- 1/2 cup celery, chopped
- 1/2 cup frozen or fresh peas
- 1/2 cup green beans
- 1/4 cup parsley, chopped
- Salt & pepper to taste

DIRECTIONS:

Place the soup bone, bay leaf, bouillon, barley, oatmeal, tomatoes, beef, thyme and paprika into 3 quarts of water in a soup kettle. Bring to a rolling boil for about 5 minutes then reduce heat and simmer for 3 hours.

Skim soup until clear while simmering. Remove soup bone. Add carrots, potatoes, celery, and beans and simmer for 30 minutes. Add peas and parsley and continue the simmer for 10 minutes.

Oats, Peas, Beans
and Barley Grow

Oats, peas, beans and barley grow,
Oats, peas, beans and barley grow,
Can you or I or anyone know
How oats, peas, beans and barley grow?

First the farmer sows his seed,
Stands erect and takes his ease,
He stamps his foot and claps his hands,
And turns around to view his lands.

Next the farmer waters the seed,
Stands erect and takes his ease,
He stamps his foot and claps his hands,
And turns around to view his lands.

Next the farmer hoes the weeds,
Stands erect and takes his ease,
He stamps his foot and claps his hands,
And turns around to view his lands.

Last the farmer harvests his seed,
Stands erect and takes his ease,
He stamps his foot and claps his hands.
And turns around to view his lands.

High Tea Main Courses

Simple Simon Pies
Mashed Potato Pie
Corny Bread Pie
Stack 'em Ups
Vegetable Cheesecake
Strata
Fritata

Simple Simon Pies

Makes 4 – 6 hand-held pies

In an area of England called Cornwall, the Cornish miners used to take a lunch called pasties to work. These are made of leftover bits of meat and potatoes with a bit of sauce in a pastry dough and baked into a hand-held lunch pie. They are very still very popular in Cornwall and other areas around the world — and they are excellent with tea for either lunch or an evening High Tea.

INGREDIENTS:

Pastry dough:

- 1 1/2 cups all purpose flour
- 1/2 teaspoon salt
- 1/2 butter or shortening
- 1 teaspoon apple cider vinegar
- Cold water as necessary
- 1 egg white, lightly beaten until just frothy

Filling:

- 1 cup cooked hamburger meat
- 1/2 cup boiled potatoes
- 1/2 cup diced onion, sautéed
- 1/2 cup cooked vegetables (carrots, celery, leek, peas, corn, etc.)
- 1/2 cup gravy or white sauce (homemade or canned)
- Salt & Pepper to taste

DIRECTIONS:

Pastry:

Sift the flour and salt together. Cut in the cold butter and vinegar. Work with a fork or pastry knife until the mixture is crumbly. Add enough cold water to make it form a dough. Knead well, about 5 minutes. Chill for 1 hour.

Preheat oven to 450 ° F.

Roll the dough thinly (about 1/4" thick) on a lightly floured board. Cut the dough into circles using a small teacup saucer as a pattern.

Filling:

Mix all the filling ingredients in a small bowl.

Scoop a serving-sized spoonful onto one half of each circle of dough. Moisten the outer edges of the circle. Gently fold over. There should be enough filling to make a nicely rounded pie. Pinch edges together or flatten together with the tines of a fork. Poke 2–3 slits in the top of the pastry. Brush with the egg white.

Bake for about 30 minutes at 450 ° F.

Option:

These pies can easily be made with other filling ingredients and can be totally vegetarian.

Simple Simon

Simple Simon met a pieman,
Going to the fair;
Says Simple Simon to the pieman,
Let me taste your ware.

Says the pieman to Simple Simon,
Show me first your penny;
Says Simple Simon to the pieman,
Indeed I have not any.

Mashed Potato Pie

Serves 4 – 6

The traditional name for this dish is Shepherd's Pie, which is often made with lamb rather than ground beef. And it is one of the dishes a family might enjoy for their evening teatime. We've made a few other changes as well.

INGREDIENTS:

Meat Filling:

- 1 onion, chopped
- 2 celery stalks, chopped
- 2 cloves garlic, minced
- 1 teaspoon dried parsley
- 1 teaspoon ground rosemary
- 1 teaspoon salt
- 2 tablespoons vegetable oil
- 3 tablespoons flour
- 1 pound lean ground beef (can also be turkey)
- 1 cup stock
- 1 cup grated cheddar or Monterey Jack cheese

Mashed Potatoes:

- 5 or 6 potatoes
- 1/4 cup milk
- 1 tablespoon butter
- Salt & pepper to taste

DIRECTIONS:

Prepare the mashed potatoes or used leftovers if you have them. Peel and quarter the potatoes. Put them in a saucepan and cover with water. Bring to a boil and cook until tender. Drain and mash. Add butter and milk and stir or whip together.

Preheat the oven to 400 ° F and grease the pie pan or baking dish.

In a skillet, heat the oil and sauté the onion, celery, garlic, parsley and rosemary until the onion is translucent. Add the ground meat, breaking it into small pieces as you add it to the pan. Stir it in thoroughly with the onion and seasonings and cook it until almost brown. Sprinkle the flour into the meat mixture and stir it in so that there are no lumps. Add the stock and simmer for 5 minutes.

Pour into the greased baking pan. Sprinkle with cheese. Top with the potatoes. Smooth potatoes over the top like a frosting. Bake for 25–30 minutes. The sauce from the filling should bubble up through holes in the potatoes.

Option:

Try the potato topping with sweet potatoes or yams.

This is a rhyme used to pick who would be it by making fists and holding them out to the person counting. Everyone says the rhyme and the counter taps each fist as well as his/her own. Each fist would be tapped once you would say each word. One word for each fist. As a fist is tapped, it is then put down, removed from the counting. At the end the person whose fist was hit last is out. They're totally out when both fists are hit.

One Potato – Two Potato

One potato, two potato, three potato, four.
Five potato, six potato, seven potato, more.

Then the person would remove the fist on the word "more" and the game would begin again.

Corny Bread Pie

Serves 4 – 6

INGREDIENTS:

Cornbread:

- 1 cup yellow cornmeal
- 1 cup all-purpose flour
- 1 tablespoon baking powder
- 1/2 teaspoon baking soda
- 3 tablespoons sugar
- 1/2 teaspoon salt
- 1 teaspoon butter (*for greasing the baking dish*)
- 1 cup buttermilk
- 1 egg
- 2 tablespoon butter melted

Filling:

- 1 lb. ground turkey
- 2 tablespoons vegetable oil
- 1 small onion
- 2 cloves garlic
- 1 cup heavy cream
- 1 beaten egg
- 1 cup grated cheddar cheese
- 1 cup fresh or frozen corn

DIRECTIONS:

Preheat oven to 350 ° F.

In a skillet, brown the turkey, onion and garlic in the vegetable oil. Drain excess oil. Set aside to cool for 10 minutes.

Mix the other filling ingredients; cream, egg, cheese and corn. Set aside.

Preheat a greased deep glass or ceramic pie pan in the oven.

In a large mixing bowl, combine the dry cornbread ingredients thoroughly. Make a well in the center of the dry mix and add the buttermilk, melted butter and egg. Mix until the egg is well blended with buttermilk then stir all ingredients together.

Melt the 1 teaspoon of butter in the hot baking dish. Pour in half of the cornbread mixture. Spoon a layer of the filling mixture gently over the bottom layer of cornbread. Gently spoon the top layer of cornbread mixture over the filling.

Bake for 40 minutes or until the top is golden brown.

Your Notes

Stack 'Em Ups

Serves 4 – 6

This is another way to use crepes.

INGREDIENTS:

Crepe Batter:

- 1 egg
- 1/2 cup milk
- 2 tablespoons club soda
- 2 tablespoons vegetable oil
- 1/2 cup all-purpose flour
- 1/4 teaspoon salt

Filling:

- 1 medium sized onion, chopped
- 2 stalks celery, chopped
- 2 cloves garlic, minced
- 1 tablespoon vegetable oil
- 1 pound ground turkey
- Salt & pepper
- 1 teaspoon paprika
- 2 cups grated Swiss cheese

Sauce:

- 2 tablespoons butter
- 2 tablespoons flour
- 1/4 cup water
- 1 cup milk
- 1 teaspoon salt
- 1 egg, beaten

DIRECTIONS:

Crepes:

Beat the egg in a medium sized bowl. Whisk in milk, club soda and oil. Gradually add flour and salt. Whisk until well blended. Cover and let the batter

rest in the refrigerator for 1/2 hour. Make 5 crepes the diameter of the cake pan or

round baking pan. The batter in the pan should be very thin. Ladle in just enough to thinly cover the bottom of the pan. Cook over medium heat for 1 1/2 minute on each side until there are beginning to show bits of brown.

Filling:

Sauté onion, celery and garlic in oil until soft. Add the turkey and break into small pieces, stirring while cooking. Season with salt, pepper and paprika – to taste. Cook until the turkey is done but not browned. Set aside to cool.

Sauce:

Melt the butter in a saucepan. Add flour and stir until all the particles of flour are completely absorbed into the melted butter. Gradually whisk in the water and then the milk. Season with salt. As the sauce begins to thicken whisk in the beaten egg until well mixed. Remove the sauce from the heat and set aside.

Assembly & Baking:

Preheat oven to 375 ° F.

Layer the crepes, filling, sauce and cheese in 4 repetitions with the sauce and cheese as the top layer on the surface of the top crepe. Bake for 20 minutes or until the top layer of sauce and cheese begin to brown. Let it cool for about 5 minutes before serving. Cut into wedges.

Vegetable Cheesecake

Serves 8 – 12

INGREDIENTS:

- 1 1/2 c. bread crumbs
- 1/2 c. butter, melted
- 2 pkgs. (8 oz.) cream cheese, softened
- 2 eggs
- 1/3 c. flour
- 1 cup sour cream
- 1 tablespoon vegetable oil
- 1/2 c. minced onion
- 2 cloves garlic, crushed
- 1 cup carrots, grated
- 1 cup zucchini, grated
- 2 tomatoes
- 2 cups grated Swiss cheese
- 1 cup additional bread crumbs

DIRECTIONS:

Preheat oven to 350 ° F.

Combine breadcrumbs and butter to form a crumb paste. Press evenly over the bottom and up the sides of spring form pan. It might stick better if the pan is lightly buttered. Chill while preparing the filling.

Beat cream cheese until fluffy. Add eggs, 1 at a time and beat in thoroughly. Add flour and sour cream. Set the cheese mixture aside.

Sauté the onion and garlic in the vegetable oil until translucent. Add the grated zucchini and carrots. Stir together and cook for 5 minutes until the vegetables begin to soften. Remove from heat.

Begin to layer the cheesecake with 1/3 of the cream cheese mixture first, topped with 1/2 the vegetable mixture and then 1/2 the grated Swiss cheese. Add another layer of the cream cheese mixture, the remainder of the vegetables and the remainder of the Swiss cheese. Finish with the last 1/3 of the cream cheese and smooth the top. Cover the top with thin slices of tomato and a layer of breadcrumbs.

Cover with aluminum foil for the first 30 minutes of baking to help cook the middle. Bake at 350 °F. Remove the foil and continue baking for 30 more minutes or until the cheesecake is done and the tomatoes on top are cooked. It is done when the center is firm to the touch and the edges begin to brown.

Your Notes

Strata

Serves 12

Have you ever had some bread that has become too dry to eat but you don't want to throw it out? You can use any bread for this recipe, even if it's a bit dry.

INGREDIENTS:

- 1 medium onion, finely chopped
- 1 medium red bell pepper, seeded and diced
- 1 clove garlic, minced
- 8 large eggs
- 4 cups milk
- 1 teaspoon salt, or to taste
- Pepper to taste
- 5 cups cubed whole-wheat country bread, crusts removed
- 1 1/2 cups grated Swiss cheese
- 1 1/2 cups diced ham
- Vegetable oil

DIRECTIONS:

Coat a 9-by-13-inch baking dish (or similar shallow 3-quart baking dish) with oil. Sauté vegetables for about 5 minutes, until softened. Add the chopped ham to the cooked vegetables after they are removed from the heat.

Whisk eggs, milk, salt and pepper in a large bowl until blended. Spread bread in the prepared baking dish. Pour ham and vegetable mixture evenly over the bread. Use a fork to combine the mixture evenly with the bread cubes Sprinkle with cheese. Cover with the egg mixture. Cover with plastic wrap and refrigerate for at least 2 hours or overnight. The bread will completely absorb the egg and the cubes will start to fall apart.

Preheat oven to 350 ° F. Bake the strata, uncovered, until puffed, lightly browned and set in the center, 55 to 65 minutes. Baking time varies greatly with the depth of the casserole dish. But you should see a bit of bubbling at the surface coming through the middle when it is done. The top will be browned and crusty.

Let cool for about 5 minutes before serving hot.

Fritata

Serves 6 – 8

Fritata is like a quiche without a piecrust. The vegetable ingredients and the cheese can be changed to your own favorites.

INGREDIENTS

- 1 medium onion, chopped
- 1 leek, trimmed, well washed and thinly sliced
- 1 garlic clove, minced
- 2 tablespoons butter or margarine
- 1/2 cup chopped tomatoes
- 1/4 cup minced fresh parsley
- 5 eggs, lightly beaten
- 2 cups shredded mozzarella cheese
- 1/2 cup soft bread crumbs
- 1/2 teaspoon salt
- 1/4 teaspoon pepper

DIRECTIONS

Preheat oven to 350°F.

In a skillet, sauté the onion, leek and garlic in butter for 5 – 10 minutes or until tender. Remove from the heat. Stir in tomatoes and parsley. Set aside.

In a large bowl, combine the remaining ingredients. Stir in reserved vegetables.

Pour into an ungreased 9-in. pie plate. Bake, uncovered, at 350°F for 30 – 35 minutes or until a knife inserted near the center comes out clean.

Let stand for 5 minutes before cutting.

Odds & Ends

At Emma Lea's Website

www.emmaleabooks.com

- *Emma Lea's Virtual Tea Party – A Monthly Newsletter*
- *Monthly Tea Story Contest*
- *Magic Teapot Stories*
- *Other Tea Activities for children, families & teachers*
- *Check for videos and interactive forums*

The Emma Lea Doll Pattern

This pattern package contains one Emma Lea Story,
the doll pattern,
sewing instructions
and dying suggestions.

The finished doll wears a child's size 5 - 6 clothes.
Dress her in your child's well-loved heirlooms or
fashions sewn from commercial patterns.

Not recommended for beginners without assistance.

Based on the Emma Lea Story Books

www.emmaleabooks.com

$10.00

44" Soft Doll Pattern

The Emma Lea Doll Story
By Babette Donaldson

Emma Lea set the table while Mama made tea and cut little cheese sandwiches and fresh apple wedges. They were going to use the fancy china plates. Emma Lea picked out their favorite teacups with matching saucers. She put a bowl of flowers in the middle of the table and then arranged her stuffed animals on the opposite side from their teacups and chairs.

Jason, the cuddly dog, snuggled up next to Theodosia Teddy Bear. Mrs. Perriwrinkle Hedgehog had a cozy place next to her husband, Mr. Perriwrinkle Hedgehog. Ginger, their real dog, was impatient for an afternoon snack. Emma Lea chose toy teacups for her pretend guests and one real plastic cup for Ginger, placed on the floor mat beside her own chair. Three china cups were set on the three flowered place mats on the table.

Mama came in with the teapot and food.

"Three places?" she asked.

"I invited Miranda to join us today."

Emma Lea ran to Mama's room to get her. Miranda stayed in the rocking chair in Mama and Daddy's room. She was Mama's old, hand-made doll. Miranda was as big as Emma Lea with wide eyes and a big smile embroidered on her soft, fabric face. She wore the special outfits that Mama had outgrown when she was Emma Lea's age. Today she was wearing a very pretty party dress.

"She loves afternoon tea with us. I'm giving her the blue cup with the dragonfly handle for today."

Emma Lea pointed to the cup chosen for her mother. "You can have your favorite hollyhock teacup. And I'll take the green one with yellow flowers, Great Grammy's first teacup when she was little."

The tea party stretched into the cool of the day. Mama handed her daughter a sweater.

162

"This is too small for me," Emma Lea laughed. "See, my arm sticks out and it's tight." The sleeves of the sweater measured how much she'd grown. "But it will fit Miranda." She put the doll's arms into the sleeves and fastened the top button at her neck. "Perfect. And it matches her dress."

After they cleared the table and washed the dishes, Mama called Grammy.

"Do you still have the doll pattern?"

Grammy knew what Mama was thinking.

"It's time to make an Emma Lea doll!" Grammy was excited. "I have just the right fabric for the body. Do we make it a surprise or an all-together-project?" Grammy asked.

"A project, of course." Mama said.

"Let's get started." Grammy suggested. "Can you come now?"

By the time they got to Grammy's house, she had smoothed the fabric out on the big table in the dining room and was gently unfolding the paper pattern pieces. Emma Lea saw the shapes of arms and legs spread out like a puzzle. Emma Lea recognized the face as Grammy unfolded it.

"Miranda. It's the Miranda pattern. Mommy's doll!"

"It's been Miranda, Meg, Miriam and Melinda. I made one for each of my girls. Now time for . . ."

"Me," Emma Lea danced with delight.

"You," Grammy smiled. "Would you like to help us?"

"Yes." Emma Lea was very happy. "Oh yes!"

She helped Grammy pin the pieces to the creamy colored fabric. She helped Mama mark the separate pieces of the doll's body with tiny notches where they would be sewn together. They followed the instructions, pinning the pieces together to form the body and then sewing each separate part together. Grammy traced the design for the face from the pattern and used her iron to transfer the lines onto the fabric. She let Emma Lea choose which pink embroidery floss she would use for the lips. A soft brown was perfect for the eyes with a darker brown for the eyelashes.

It was almost to dinnertime.

"I'll embroider the face tonight," Grammy said. "We can finish the head tomorrow."

Emma Lea and Mama were at Grammy's house early the next morning after a stop at the craft store. They had the yarn for hair, a color almost like Emma Lea's. When Emma Lea went to the table, the face piece was already smiling back at her. Grammy had embroidered brown eyes and a wide, pink smile. It was ready to sew together.

They had it almost finished before lunch. Arms and legs were thick. The head was round and full. The body was waiting to have everything attached and they had made a lot of very long brown hair by wrapping the yarn around a piece of cardboard, taping it in place and then sewing it to make it all stay together. Grampop came in as they were braiding the soft, yarn hair.

"My gracious," he said, "it looks just like you."

Mama helped Emma Lea dress the doll in an outfit Emma Lea had just outgrown. Her favorite. A special party dress with lots of frills. Emma Lea squealed with delight. "She does look like me."

"Just in time," Grammy's eyes twinkled as she looked out the window.

Aunt Meg, Aunt Melinda, Aunt Miriam had arrived with their own dolls. Mama got her Miranda doll and they all stayed for tea.

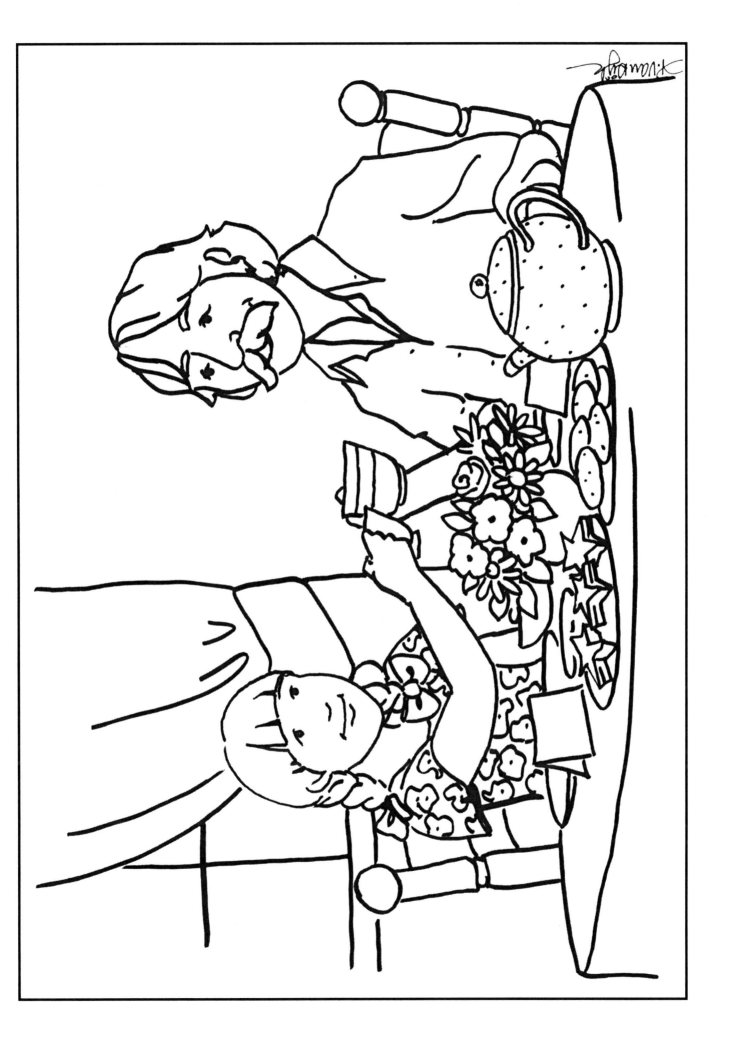

The Emma Lea Books

"Tea is for everyone!" Emma Lea transforms a ladies-only family tradition to include the entire family. EMMA LEA'S FIRST TEA PARTY, the first book in the series introduces the entire family and an annual tea party celebration for Grammy's birthday.

In, EMMA LEA'S MAGIC TEAPOT, Emma Lea dreams her new teapot is as magic as Aladdin's Lamp. Her friend Sam and her family help her understand that the real magic in the world isn't in objects. It is in the power of their relationships.

Her friend Sam shares his family's tradition of Japanese style tea in EMMA LEA'S FIRST TEA CEREMONY. She learns about tea traditions around the world. But as she does, she comes to understand and appreciate her own family traditions even more.

Emma lea creates a special tea lunch for her father in EMMA LEA'S TEA WITH DADDY After a day of chores she shares the secret of afternoon teatime. "We just talk. I tell you what's happening at school. You tell me about your work. Or what you did when you were a little boy. You know. The things that matter."

About this cookbook

The recipes in this cookbook are taken from one of the Emma Lea Stories: from the storybooks pictured here and also in the Magic Teapot Stories on our website and in Emma Lea's Tea-Zine, a free monthly newsletter. In most stories, Emma Lea and her friends share the fun of preparing food and tea. Many of the recipes are inspired by songs nursery rhymes to help build a theme for a party. Some become activities or games. Almost all of them require the supervision and assistance of an adult. But in each one there is an important task for a young child.

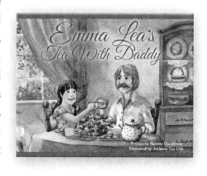

I believe we can help children choose tea as a healthy alternative to canned and heavily sweetened drinks by making teatime special and fun. Teatime can become a nurturing tradition for everyone.

Babette Donaldson
Author of The Emma Lea Books

For more about the
Emma Lea books and stories,
visit our website:

www.emmaleabooks.com.

173

174

Breinigsville, PA USA
16 January 2011
253356BV00003B/2/P